Greenhill Books

SUBMACHINE GUNS

GREENHILL MILITARY MANUALS

SUBMACHINE GUNS

GREENHILL MILITARY MANUALS

Ian V. Hogg

Greenhill Books, London
Stackpole Books, Pennsylvania

Greenhill Books

Submachine Guns first published 2001 by
Greenhill Books, Lionel Leventhal Limited, Park House, 1 Russell Gardens, London NW11 9NN
and
Stackpole Books, 5067 Ritter Road, Mechanicsburg, PA 17055, USA

British Library Cataloguing in Publication Data

Hogg, Ian V. (Ian Vernon), 1926-
Submachine guns. – (Greenhill military manuals)
1. Submachine guns – History
1. Title
623.4'424

ISBN 1-85367-448-6

Library of Congress Cataloging-in-Publication Data Available

Design and layout by John Anastasio
Printed and bound in Singapore

Front cover illustration: P90 Personal Defence Weapon. By courtesy F.N. Herstal S.A.

Contents

INTRODUCTION

The submachine gun as a military weapon is definitely a weapon of the twentieth century; it was born in World War One, came to its zenith in World War Two, and was then gradually ousted from its position by the assault rifle. By the end of the century it was no longer a front-line weapon in any major army, being restricted to use by military police and rear-echelon troops. As a police weapon, though, it still has a role to play and there is no doubt that in the counter-terrorist battle it will be a major tool for years to come.

The submachine gun appeared rather in the nature of a solution seeking a problem; the first weapon which really qualified as a submachine gun (and we will look at the criteria in a moment) was designed and developed by Hugo Schmeisser, a German engineer who was chief designer for the Theodor Bergmann Company of Berlin. Some time in early 1916 it seems that he took a hard look at the way the war was going and asked himself what sort of weapon might be needed to crack the trench stalemate. It was about this time, too, that Colonel Hutier and General Ludendorff were experimenting with new tactical theories on the Eastern Front which were to lead to

Everybody knows about the German rifle that fired round corners; not many people know that the British had a submachine gun that did the same thing. This Sten is hinged at the butt and has a prism sight.

the Storm Troops and the tactics of infiltration. Bergmann reasoned that what was needed to augment this was a compact, fast-firing, short-range weapon, and he set about developing what became known as the Bergmann *Muskete* (musket) or *Kugelspritz* (literally 'bullet-squirter'), or more formally, the *Maschinenpistole* 18. There is a record of the interrogation of a German soldier taken prisoner by the British in June 1916 in which he describes a 'new Bergmann pistol' which had been issued in limited numbers for trial and his description corresponds in its details with the characteristics of the Bergmann MP18. The troops appear to have been enthusiastic but it took time to persuade the higher echelons who controlled the purse strings and it was not until the latter part of 1917 that the first service issues were made.

By that time the other contender for the title of 'first submachine gun' was being used by the Italian Army, but in a totally different tactical concept. Here the Italian Army, fighting in the Alps, wanted a light machine-gun with a very high rate of fire for relatively short range work conducted by their specialist Alpine troops. And the Villar Perosa engineering company produced a twin-gun system, two small blowback machine-guns mounted side by side, magazine fed, firing the 9mm Glisenti pistol cartridge, and carried on a frame suspended from the gunner's shoulders rather in the manner of a match-seller's tray. This was the Villar Perosa machine-gun and because it appeared in 1915, was a blowback system and fired pistol ammunition it is often claimed as the first submachine gun. So let us now look at the accepted definition of a submachine gun.

There are any number of definitions of submachine guns, in fact; unfortunately you can invariably find something which is undoubtedly a submachine gun but which fails in one or more of the criteria in every definition. The one fixed feature was always that it fired pistol ammunition; but even this has been overturned in recent years. Indeed, since the 1950s the Soviet Union, its satellites and their successors invariably called the Kalashnikov rifles 'submachine guns'. In more recent years weapons chambered for the 5.45mm, and 5.56mm rifle cartridges have been marketed as submachine guns, and even one firing the standard 7.62x51mm NATO rifle cartridge. Historically, then, the definition has been as follows:

• it is a short-range weapon
• it fires a pistol cartridge
• it is an automatic weapon
• it is a blowback weapon
• it is a light weapon
• it can be fired from the shoulder or the hip and demands both hands.

And that is, really, about as far as one should go; some people try and define it in tactical terms as a self-defence weapon, but this flies in the face of tens of thousands of Soviet soldiers in World War Two who used it very effectively as an offensive weapon. Indeed, the 'Personal Defence Weapon' has begun to appear as the military successor to the submachine gun, but we will examine that a little later. But having drawn up the above definition it would be very easy to produce a list of weapons which fail to meet all the desired features and yet are still considered to be submachine guns. In the end, if it looks like a submachine gun, fires like a submachine gun and handles like a submachine gun, it is a submachine gun.

Bergmann's *Muskete* obviously qualifies as a submachine gun under the features listed above, its tactical use and as a handy source of intense firepower for individual soldiers. The Villar Perosa (V-P), on the other hand, although meeting the mechanical criteria, was actually used as a squad light machine-gun in the supporting role, not in the sort of short-range hurly-burly with which one usually associates submachine guns. In fact, it was so ill-suited to being any sort of machine-gun that in 1918 the twin guns were removed from their mountings, separated and fitted into wooden stocks to become real submachine guns.

Strangely, the Bergmann and the V-P made little post-war impact on the victorious powers. The Bergmann was forbidden to the revived German Army but permitted to the German civil police, while the V-P and its derivatives, the Beretta and the OVP, were completely ignored. It was left to General John T. Thompson to bring this class of weapon into the public eye and to coin the term 'submachine gun'.

Thompson had been dealing with small arms for most of his military career and he retired in 1914 with the intention of developing an automatic rifle. This, of course, demanded a locked breech, and he settled on the Blish System of

The L34A1 Sterling as a silent sniping weapon, shown here in the hands of a Royal Marine Commando.

slipping inclined faces: in brief, the bolt is locked to the receiver by a wedge and the faces of the two are at such an angle that under high pressure they stick together but when the pressure drops they slide apart and the bolt opens. A dubious system at the best of times, it was soon found to be a failure with high-powered rifle cartridges, but Oscar Payne, Thompson's designer-draughtsman, tried it with a .45 pistol cartridge and found it worked beautifully. On hearing this, Thompson made a lightning decision to forget the rifle and turn it into what he called a 'Trench Broom' for close-quarter fighting. But by that time, he had returned to the army and was supervising the mass-production of Enfield rifles in the USA, so it was not until after the war that he was able to devote time to perfecting the idea, inventing, in the process, the term 'submachine gun'. He got Colt to manufacture a few thousand guns, then spent the next fifteen or so years selling them in penny packets here and there to police forces, the US Marines and, being a somewhat naive man, to gangsters and the Irish Republican Army, all of which garnered immense publicity and got the weapon the reputation for being a somewhat irregular, underhand, vulgar 'gangster's gun'.

In Europe the only moves of any significance in the 1920s were that Bergmann made some improvements to his MP18 and turned it into the MP28, while a Finnish designer called Aimo Lahti took Bergmann's design, made some changes and improvements of his own and produced what he called the 'Suomi' (which is the Finnish word for Finland) SMG. Beretta began looking at their 1918 design and made some improvements in the 1930s and the Soviets, never ones to miss any opportunity and, unlike all the western nations, never short of money to spend on armaments, tried out one or two weapons submitted by various designers. In general, all these inter-war submachine guns were similar – expensively made by machining the parts from solid metal and fitted with well-shaped and polished wooden butts, they all showed a resemblance to the original Bergmann in one way or another.

By the mid-1930s tension in Europe was building up and Germany was rearming. Among the several innovations that the German *Wehrmacht* was introducing was mechanised infantry, the successors to the Storm Troopers, and if these men were to be packed into vehicles and enter and leave them quickly, they needed a compact weapon. A few submachine guns were adopted, but the *Wehrmacht* was not sure that the designs met its requirements. Berthold Geipel of the Erfurt Machinery Works sat down with Vollmer, his designer, and between them they arrived at an entirely new concept of weapon. It was all metal, with a machined receiver, several stamped parts and a folding metal butt. With this folded, the entire weapon was just over two-thirds the length of the Bergmann and half the length of the standard Mauser Kar 98k rifle. This was offered to the *Wehrmacht* which promptly took it into service as the Machine Pistol 38. It virtually became the *Wehrmacht* trademark.

The submachine gun (here, an H&K MP5) is the preferred weapon of special forces and counter-terrorist teams across the world.

The 1930s saw a number of small wars, notably the Gran Chaco War of 1932–5, the Sino-Japanese War of 1931–41 and, of course, the Spanish Civil War of 1936–9. These have been credited with fostering the growth of the submachine gun. The facts are against this; recent research has shown that less than 4000 submachine guns reached Spain during the Civil War – compared to half a million rifles from Russia alone – and no memoir even mentions such weapons. The Japanese completely ignored the submachine gun, and there is equally little confirmation for any major use of the submachine gun in the South American affair. It was, in the eyes of many soldiers of many nations, a remedy looking for a disease. It did not fit into any of the preconceived tactical theories of the day (except in Germany and to a lesser extent in Russia) and it was therefore better to ignore it. Fortunately, this did not extend to the technical staffs; thus, when war broke out in 1939, the British Army was able to say that it had, over the past few years, tested about a dozen submachine guns, that the best, in its opinion, was the Suomi, but that the only one available in any quantity was the Thompson, which was also the most expensive – all of $45.

By the late spring of 1940 it had become obvious that whatever shape the war was going to take, it was not the shape of 1914–18 and more fluid sorts of tactics were needed. And in the wake of the German conquest of Norway, Denmark, the Low Countries and finally France, the British suddenly realised that the cheap and easily made submachine gun was a very desirable property. The Russians, confronted with well-handled Suomi guns in the Finnish forests during the Winter War, came to a similar conclusion. The British, to save time, decided to adopt an existing design and went for the Bergmann MP28. This accorded well with the British manner of gunmaking, with plenty of machining, a nice wooden stock and lots of scope for brasswork around the magazine housing. Fortunately, while preparations for the production of this weapon were still being made, two inventors appeared with a cheap and effective alternative. The War Office was wise enough to forget tradition and go for the cost-effective solution, and the Sten gun was born.

By 1942, submachine gun designs were coming thick and fast, notably in the USA where several weapons were striving for military adoption. Most were in the same idiom as the Thompson, with machined receivers, elegant wooden stock and fore-grips, elegant weapons in every respect save one – they were not designed for rapid mass-production. Eventually the US Army tired of testing these weapons, obtained a Sten gun from the British, sat its designers down in front of it and demanded something similar. This resulted in the Grease Gun – the Submachine Gun M3 – as cheap and simple as the Sten and rather more attractive in appearance. As with the Sten, the purists shuddered, but it did the business.

The Russians had also simplified their designs down to the minimum, producing weapons which, when casually examined, appeared to be wretched constructions of stamped metal and welding. When more closely scrutinised, though, it became apparent that where a high degree of finish was necessary for the reliable functioning of the weapon, it was there; where a high degree of finish was merely a cosmetic addition, it was absent. With these weapons arming their 'Tank Riders' they fought their way across Europe. The submachine gun accorded well with the Soviet tactics: not for them a long-range exchange of fire, but a charge into battle on the back of a tank, to leap off and get among the enemy at short range where even a hastily trained conscript could hardly miss.

By the time the war ended in 1945 the world was awash with submachine guns. The British had turned out the Sten by the million and distributed it wholesale across the clandestine forces of Europe. The Russians had mass-produced three different models, also by the million. The Germans had turned out the MP38 and its cheaper successor the MP40, as well as other designs. The Australians had made the Austen and the Owen, the Americans the Thompson as designed by Thompson and also a modified and

simplified version, the M3 and a few others, the Japanese had finally got around to making one and the Italians had revamped the Beretta designs. And those were only the official weapons. There were also plenty of designers working away merrily on new models and there were also clandestine workshops producing copies of the Sten for use by resistance and guerrilla groups. All these designs, with the possible exception of the original Thompson, were remarkably similar in their operation. They were blowback weapons, relying upon a heavy bolt with a return spring to keep the breech closed until the bullet was clear of the muzzle. Most of them used a fixed firing pin to fire the cartridge while the bolt was still closing, so that the explosive force had first to arrest the bolt, then reverse its movement and blow it back. By taking advantage of this 'advanced primer ignition' feature, the weight and bulk of the bolt could be kept lower than was possible in designs in which the bolt came to rest before firing. The barrels were short – the bullet had to be out before the breech started opening – and the guns were relatively long because there had to be room for the bolt to move back and forth behind the barrel. But as the frenzy of war began to subside, so people had time to stop and contemplate

The Sten gun was widely distributed during the war; this is a French Maquisard with a Mark 2 which had been dropped by parachute.

the design of their weapons and question whether this conventional layout was, indeed, the only way to go.

In fact, the first piece of original thinking had taken place in Italy in 1942 when Giovanni Oliani, an engineer working for the Fabbrica de Armas de Guerra of Cremona, invented the overhung breechblock. Instead of having a massive cylindrical block behind the barrel, Oliani's breechblock was quite small, just large enough to carry the firing pin and withstand the explosive force of the cartridge, but it was attached to a much larger piece of metal which lay in a tube above the barrel of the gun. This piece of metal gave the bolt the **11** desired weight to withstand premature opening, but because the bulk was in front of the breech face, the distance behind the barrel which the bolt travelled on the loading cycle was less than half that which would be needed in a conventional layout. So Oliani had two choices: he could make his barrel longer (and thus get better velocity and range) or make his entire gun shorter. What he actually did was a bit of both, but by the time he got the thing working properly in 1944 there was not much of a future in designing submachine guns in Italy, so he never got beyond a couple of prototype models.

The first major use of submachine guns came in the 1939–40 Winter War when the Finns made their forests death traps for the Soviet Army.

Word gets round in the ordnance business and Oliani's idea came to rest in Czechoslovakia where it went through a slight change of shape to become the 'telescoped bolt'. The principle remained the same – get the bulk of the bolt out in front of the bolt face – but the method of achieving it was rather more elegant. The telescoped bolt can best be described as follows. An ordinary bolt is made, somewhat oversize, then a deep hole is drilled into the face. At the bottom of this hole a new bolt face and firing pin are made. The barrel is then mounted within the receiver so that it sticks into the receiver as an unsupported tube. When the bolt goes forward, the breech end of the barrel enters the hole in the bolt until the new bolt face reaches the breech. At that point, with the bolt closed, more of the bolt overhangs the barrel than is behind it, so that although the necessary weight is there, the amount of metal behind the breech is very small and the amount of recoil travel is correspondingly reduced. There are obvious complications. Slots and holes have to be cut into the bolt in order to permit feed and ejection, though this is rather simpler than might be thought. Another result of this construction is that since the bolt travel is short, the receiver is correspondingly short, and the pistol grip comes forward until it can be wrapped around the magazine. This is highly advantageous when it comes to changing magazines in the dark because one hand can always find the other.

This conjunction of features appeared in 1948 in a design by Vaclav Holek, the man who had designed the famous Bren light machine-gun, and it set a new standard for compactness. It was introduced as the CZ23 and gave rise to four variant models, described elsewhere. It also made designers stop and think, suggesting that there might be other ways of designing a submachine gun other than simply following in Schmeisser's footsteps. It also stimulated some designers to take the basic concept of the telescoped bolt and central magazine and improve it. One result of such thinking was the Uzi submachine gun produced in Israel and subsequently used throughout the world.

The first suggestion that the submachine gun might be supplanted by another weapon came with the Soviet adoption of the Kalashnikov AK47 rifle. This fired a short 7.62mm cartridge and hence was a compact rifle. With a folding butt it was as convenient to carry as many submachine guns, so much so that by the mid-1950s the Soviet Army and its satellites had discarded the wartime submachine guns and equipped their troops entirely with the AK rifles. But, strangely enough, they still called them 'submachine guns' and continued to do so for many years, causing no end of confusion among Western intelligence agencies.

In the period 1945–60 a considerable number of submachine gun designs were put forward by inventors to armies around the world; they were attractive because they were relatively simple to make. A successful design could look forward to being sold in large numbers. But few of them paid much attention to the lessons of the CZ23 and were very much in the pre-war mould, machined from solid steel with elegant polished wooden butts and optimistic sights. Others went too far in the other direction and resembled a gas-fitter's nightmare. A few tried to be original; one French designer produced a weapon in which the bolt was controlled by a flywheel, another produced a design in which every component telescoped or folded into another until the whole thing was capable of fitting into a large pocket. The only trouble was that by the time you had unfolded it and got it into working order, the war was over.

A notable feature of this rash of post-war design was that it settled the calibre question: the guns were almost all in 9mm Parabellum and those that were not 9mm were firing the .45 ACP cartridge. The pre-war (in the case of

The submachine gun is an ideal weapon for women; these are members of the South African Defence Force getting in some practice with their Uzis.

Russia, wartime) calibre of 7.63mm Mauser was abandoned, as was the 9mm Mauser Export, the 9mm Steyr and the 9mm Browning Long, all of which had been offered before 1939. The Spanish still clung to their 9mm Largo (also called Bergmann-Bayard) and the Czechs had a rush of blood to the head and built their Skorpion in 7.65mm Browning calibre, but these were exceptions. What often seems remarkable to the layman is that very few people tried to take advantage of a wartime-developed cartridge which, on the face of it, appeared to be ideal for the role – the US .30 carbine round.

Those people who did try soon ran into a fundamental problem which was to reappear some years later in another context: the .30 carbine cartridge was designed specifically for the .30 carbine, which had a barrel 18in long. To obtain ballistic consistency, cartridges are designed to burn all their propellant well before the bullet reaches the muzzle and a point about two-third of the way up the bore is generally chosen as the ideal 'all-burnt' point, leaving a short length of bore in which the bullet settles down to a consistent velocity. In the case of the .30 carbine, this meant that the powder burned out after the bullet had travelled about 12in. And since submachine guns almost always have barrels of less than 12in, the weapons which tried to use the .30 round were notorious for spewing out burning powder behind the bullet, leading to vivid flash, totally random velocities and gross inaccuracy.

With the general adoption of small calibre (5.56mm and the like) assault rifles after the 1960s, it looked as if the days of the submachine gun were numbered, as army after army discarded them in favour of the small rifle. But then came the rise of terrorism and a greater readiness of the criminal element to adopt automatic weapons. As a result, the police forces of the world began to think about improving their armouries and the submachine gun appeared to be the ideal weapon. It was convenient to carry, held plenty of ammunition, could be fired from the shoulder, giving a better chance of a hit than free-hand pistol shooting, and fired a short-range bullet which had a great deal less likelihood of ricocheting off a wall and killing some innocent bystander than did a high-velocity rifle bullet.

This demand led to a new batch of designs, of which perhaps the most successful and widely used is the Heckler & Koch MP5 and its variations. This has the advantage of using an existing breech closure system taken

from the company's rifles, in which the breech closes but the weapon does not fire until a hammer is released. This means that the first shot can be fired with much greater accuracy than with the usual type of submachine gun firing 'from an open bolt'. With an open bolt, the gun is cocked and ready to fire with the chamber empty and the bolt held back by the sear. When the firer presses the trigger the bolt flies forward, collects a cartridge from the magazine, thrusts it into the chamber, then fires it. Now, all that takes a finite amount of time, short though it may be, and the shift in balance as the bolt runs forward invariably shifts the weapon off the point of aim. Consequently, while the first round might well land somewhere in the general area of the aiming point, it is pure fluke if it actually hits what the firer has aimed at. But the MP5 firing 'from a closed bolt' does not suffer from this defect and, given the requisite skill on the part of the firer, puts the first round where it is wanted. Which is why the gun is particularly favoured by special forces and hostage rescue teams.

Another drawback to the submachine gun, in the eyes of policemen, was that unless you carried it cocked, there was always some delay when you were called upon to fire. It had to be cocked first, then brought up to the aim, by which time

The current move is to the Personal Defence Weapon, a light but powerful submachine gun which can be carried by those troops who do not require a full-powered assault rifle for their daily tasks.

the terrorist might well have got his shot in first. An Italian design, the Spectre, overcame this defect by giving the submachine gun the same double-action trigger mechanism as the revolver or the modern automatic pistol. The weapon can be carried loaded, with the bolt closed and the hammer lowered into a safe position; when the need arises, all the firer has to do is pull the trigger to cock and release the hammer.

The next revolution came in the early 1980s when it was discovered that the Russians had developed a submachine gun firing their 5.45mm rifle cartridge. They had obviously run into the same problems as those people who had tried to build a weapon around the .30 carbine cartridge twenty years before. The Soviet 5.45x39.6mm cartridge was optimised for a 15.75in barrel; the AK-74-SU submachine gun had a 8.1in barrel, but was fitted with an expansion chamber-cum-flash-hider which allowed the gases to stabilise outside the muzzle but concealed them from view, reducing the flash, improving the consistency and also balancing the gas pressure so that the action of the weapon was less violent than would otherwise have been the case. This, of course, led to a rash of designs for 5.56mm submachine guns, but generally speaking these were less well thought out and lacked the vital expansion chamber, with the result that their flash and muzzle blast were excessive. The only good 5 56mm submachine guns are actually better described as short-barrelled assault rifles.

But it was becoming important to develop a more powerful cartridge for the submachine gun, since body armour was now commonplace on the battlefield and in the streets and the 9mm Parabellum was the one cartridge that most body armour was designed to beat. And body armour which could stop 9mm Parabellum would also stop any other submachine gun calibre rounds, such as .40 or .45.

Another consideration, which was beginning to be understood in some armies, was the question of how their troops should be armed. Modern firearms, particularly assault rifles, are expensive. About four-fifths of the personnel of an army do not really need an assault rifle because they are going to be cooking stew, driving trucks, counting shirts and boots, typing out company orders and doing all the household chores of which there are always plenty in any army. So why give them an expensive and specialised weapon which they will never need? But they do need to be able to defend themselves if the worst comes to the worst. On the other hand, you cannot give them all pistols, since nine-tenths of them would never have time to practise which is essential if you hope to hit anything with a pistol. And the submachine gun was fast becoming out of date, incapable of defeating the body armour and helmets which an enemy would undoubtedly be wearing.

FN of Belgium, a far-sighted company with a record of innovative designs, looked at this problem and came up with a solution: the P90 submachine gun, a futuristic design which fires a 5.7mm bullet at high velocity (for such a weapon) and can defeat body armour at combat ranges with the standard ball bullet; an armour piercing bullet has been designed but is not yet a necessity. They also coined a new term to describe the gun – Personal Defence Weapon, or PDW. Armies have looked at the logic and found it sound. Several have now begun research into their own design of PDW while others are content to go to FN with their chequebooks. It seems probable that the 5.7mm cartridge developed with the P90 will become a standard design, since it is now in use in an FN pistol and there are moves afoot to standardise it as a NATO calibre.

And so we have reached the start of the twenty-first century with the submachine gun still very much with us and in the process of making another change of direction. Twenty years ago we were freely prophesying that by the end of the twentieth century the weapon would be history, but circumstances alter cases and there is every possibility that the new century will see the resurgence of the submachine gun, in the guise of the Personal Defence Weapon as a military arm.

When the Pacific War started in 1941, Australia was desperately short of modern weapons; Britain was in no position to supply any – being in dire straits herself – and so the Australians set about producing their own, with only a limited amount of machinery and plant. Designs had therefore to be both straightforward and easy to manufacture. Submachine guns were urgently needed for the jungle campaigns and the Austen combined features of the Sten and the German MP40 *(see below)*. The receiver, barrel, trigger mechanism and bolt were of Sten design, but the MP40 was the model for the main spring, folding stock and sloping pistol grip. The resulting weapon had few vices except for the inherited Sten difficulty with feed and a combined trigger and sear spring which had a tendency to break. The Austen went into production in mid-1942, some months after the Owen gun *(see below)* entered service, and by April 1943 only 4000 or so had been made, the rate of production being about one-third that of the Owen. As a result, the Owen was officially declared to be the Australian service weapon and the Austen, although apparently allowed to continue in production until the war ended, was never used in any numbers.

The Austen Mark II was produced only in limited numbers in 1944–5 and differed principally from the Mark I in having a two-piece cast aluminium receiver and frame.

Cartridge 9mm Parabellum
Length *stock extended* 33.25in (845mm) *stock retracted* 21.75in (552mm)
Weight *Mark I* 8lb 12oz (3.97kg) *Mark II* 8lb 8oz (3.85kg)
Barrel 7.80in (198mm), 6 grooves, right-hand twist
Magazine 28-round box
Muzzle velocity 1200ft/sec (366m/sec)
Cyclic rate 500rds/min
Manufacturers Diecasters Ltd, Melbourne, Victoria; W.T. Carmichael & Co., Melbourne, Victoria

(Right) Austen Mark 1, a combination of Sten and MP40 features.

(Right) Austen Mark 2 was the same gun but clad in a cast aluminium receiver.

This weapon was developed by Evelyn Owen in .22 calibre in June 1939, and he offered it to the Australian Army without raising much interest. On the outbreak of war he was called up into the army and left the gun and details with a friend who managed to spur the Army Inventions Board into asking Lysaghts, in January 1941, to manufacture a prototype in .32 ACP

calibre. The Australian Army were then awaiting supplies of the Sten *(see below)*, but after some delay decided to purchase 100 Owen guns in .38 calibre, the necessary design work being done by G.S. Wardell, chief engineer of Lysaghts. A pilot model of this was made in August 1941 and proved that the British .38 revolver round was useless as a submachine gun cartridge.

Lysaghts, on their own responsibility, changed the design to 9mm Parabellum. The prototype was tested against the Thompson *(see below)* and Sten, proved superior to both and went into production. Due to a shortage of machine tools it was not until mid-1942 that full production of 2000 per month was achieved and thereafter production was held at this rate solely by the

The Owen gun was usually painted in camouflage colours. The knob in front of the magazine is to release the barrel.

availability of tooling. Although the US Army in Australia wanted to purchase 60,000 Owen guns, the proposal was refused by the Australian authorities since they could not find the necessary materials and machine tools.

The Owen was a simple blowback weapon with two odd features: the overhead feeding magazine and a separate bolt compartment inside the receiver, so that the bolt was isolated from its cocking handle by a small bulkhead. This ensured that the bolt could not be jammed by dirt or mud, though it was expensive in terms of space. Two other unusual features were that the ejector was built into the magazine, rather than into the gun, and the barrel could be removed quickly by pulling up on a spring-loaded plunger, necessary because the gun could only be stripped by removing the barrel and taking the bolt out forwards.

Three models of Owen were made; the Mark I (or 1/42) which went through several minor modifications; the Mark I Wood Butt (or 1/43); and the Mark II which was a simplified model and only produced in prototype in 1943. It had a different method of attaching the stock and had a bayonet lug above the muzzle compensator to receiver a special tubular-haft bayonet.

Total production amounted to about 45,000 before Lysaghts ended manufacture in September 1945. The Owen remained in use until the 1960s and numbers are still held in reserve stores.

Cartridge 9x19mm Parabellum
Length 32.0in (813mm)
Weight *Mark I* 9lb 5oz (4.21kg)
  Mark II 7lb 10oz (3.47kg)
Barrel 9.75in (247mm), 7 grooves, right-hand twist
Magazine 33-round box
Muzzle velocity 1378ft/sec (420m/sec)
Cyclic rate 700rds/min
Manufacturer Lysaght's Newcastle Works Pty Ltd, Port Kembla, NSW

An unpainted Owen with the magazine removed; the magazine does not rely on gravity – the gun fires equally well upside down.

19

Steyr MPi 69

Austria

The MPi 69 was developed by Steyr, having been designed by Herr Stowasser, with the objectives of reliability and cheap manufacture firmly in view. The receiver is a steel pressing with a molded nylon cover and much of the assembly of components is by welding and brazing. The barrel is cold-hammered by a Steyr-developed process which produces a cleaner rifling contour and tougher barrel at less expense than the usual system of boring and rifling. The machined bolt is 'overhung' or 'wrap-around' in form, in which the bolt face is about halfway along the length of the bolt body, allowing a large mass to lie around the barrel and also permitting the use of a barrel somewhat longer than normal while keeping the overall length of the weapon within reasonable bounds.

The selection of single shot or automatic fire is achieved by pressure on the trigger; a light pressure produces single shots, while heavier pressure brings in a locking device which holds down the sear and permits automatic fire. An additional control is provided in the safety catch; this is a cross-bolt type, pushed to the right with the thumb to make the weapon safe and pushed to the left with the forefinger to ready the weapon for firing. If the bolt is pushed only halfway through its travel, the mechanism is locked so that only single shots can be fired. The gun is cocked by pulling on the carrying sling – the front end of the sling is attached to the bolt. A telescoping wire stock is fitted.

Cartridge 9x19mm Parabellum
Length *stock extended* 26.38in (670mm) *stock retracted* 18.31in (465mm)
Weight 6lb 14oz (3.13kg)
Barrel 10.24in (260mm), 6 grooves, right-hand twist
Magazine 25- or 32-round box
Muzzle velocity 1250ft/sec (381m/sec)
Cyclic rate 550rds/min
Manufacturer Steyr-Mannlicher GmbH, Steyr

The MPi 69, a neat and well-balanced design.

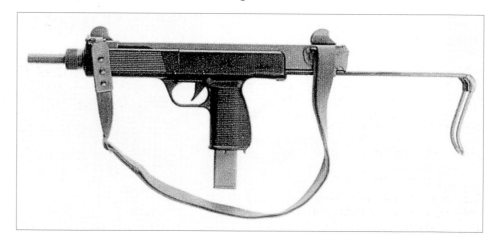

Steyr MPi 81

The MPi 69 *(see above)* has a unique cocking system in which the sling is connected to the bolt and used to cock the weapon. Some purchasers did not like this system so Steyr modified the design in 1980 to use a conventional cocking handle. This version is known as the MPi 81. In all other respects it is identical with the MPi 69.

A special version of the MPi 81 was developed as a firing-port weapon for use in infantry fighting vehicles and similar vehicles fitted with firing ports for the occupants. The receiver is fitted with the optical sight of the AUG rifle; the barrel is extended and fitted with a special collar which locks into the standard pattern of firing port. The sight is positioned by a special bracket so that it can be used with the vision blocks fitted above the firing ports.

The MPi 69 stripped; note the length of barrel inside the receiver and the telescoped bolt.

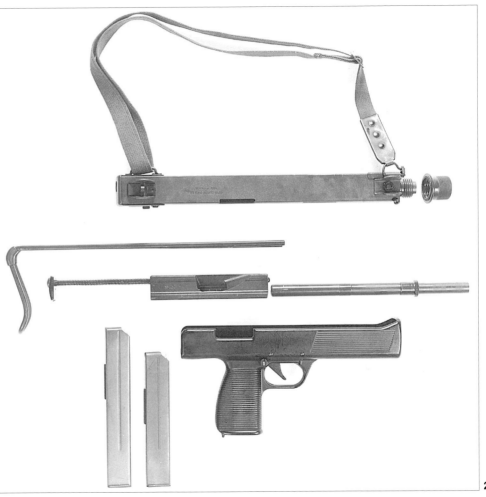

21

Steyr AUG-9 Austria

This is a submachine gun version of the standard AUG assault rifle, introduced in 1986. It uses the existing stock and receiver units of the rifle, with carrying handle and optical sight, but is fitted with a 9mm calibre barrel, a special blowback bolt group, a magazine adapter and a magazine. The adapter fits into the normal 5.56mm magazine housing in the stock, and the 9mm magazine then fits into the adapter. As with the AUG rifle, its parent weapon, the carrying handle and receiver can be exchanged for a version which, instead of the optical sight, has a flat platform to which any standard optical or electro-optical sight can be fitted. It is also one of the few submachine guns from which grenades can be launched. The barrel may be removed and replaced with one carrying an integral silencer.

Cartridge 9x19mm Parabellum
Length 26.18in (665mm)
Weight 7lb 5oz (3.30kg)
Barrel 16.54in (420mm), 6 grooves, right-hand twist
Magazine 25- or 32-round box
Muzzle velocity 1312ft/sec (400m/sec)
Cyclic rate 700rds/min
Manufacturer Steyr-Mannlicher GmbH, Steyr

The Steyr AUG-9 Para, derived from an assault rifle, complete with silencer and an optical sight in the carrying handle.

Compact firepower: the AUG-9 Para can also launch grenades.

The TMP (Tactical Machine Pistol), introduced in 1989, consists of a synthetic butt and frame, synthetic receiver top, and a steel barrel and breechblock combination. It is hammer fired, the firing mechanism being modified from that of the AUG rifle. The weapon works on the delayed blowback principle, the delay being preformed by a rotating barrel which owes a good deal to the Steyr 1912 pistol. The barrel lies inside a casing which fits into the top cover and acts as a guide for the bolt. On firing, bolt and barrel recoil 12mm, then a lug on the barrel, having moved down a slot, hits a cam surface and rotates the barrel about 45° clockwise. This unlocks the bolt; the barrel stops and the bolt continues rearwards. A spring drives the bolt back to collect a fresh round and chamber it, then drives the bolt into the battery. Semi-auto or auto fire can be selected by cross-bolt safety/selector or by trigger pressure as on the MPi 69 (see above). There are forty-one parts and only one screw, the lateral adjustment for the rear sight. There is no stock, but a grip in front of the trigger guard can be folded down to give a two-hand hold.

Cartridge 9x19mm Parabellum
Length 11.10in (282mm)
Weight 2lb 14oz (1.30kg)
Barrel 5.12in (130mm), 6 grooves, right-hand twist

Magazine 15- or 30-round box
Muzzle velocity 1180ft/sec (360m/sec)
Cyclic rate 900rds/min
Manufacturer Steyr-Mannlicher GmbH, Steyr

The Steyr TMP is largely made of synthetic materials and relies on a rotating barrel to lock the breech.

23

Steyr-Solothurn MP34   Austria

The history of this weapon shows the lengths to which German companies went to in order to get round the restrictions of the Versailles Treaty in the 1920–34 period. Manufacture of submachine guns was forbidden to German firms; design, however, was not. Rheinmetall designed this weapon, then passed the designs to a Swiss subsidiary, the Waffenfabrik Solothurn AG who made the prototypes, carried out the testing and made whatever modifications were necessary. The prototype and manufacturing drawings then went to the Waffenfabrik Steyr in Austria where the guns were manufactured. The weapon was adopted by the Austrian and Hungarian armies and sold widely in South America and the Far East. It was also bought by Portugal in 1935; the Portuguese *Guarda Fiscal* were still using them into the mid-1970s. Manufacture ceased in 1940. Although the official submachine gun of the German Army was the MP40 *(see below)*, the Solothurn was issued in quite large numbers as the *Maschinenpistole* 34(ö) and remained in service until 1945.

The Steyr-Solothurn is, without doubt, the Rolls-Royce of submachine guns; machined from solid steel throughout, the quality and finish are perhaps the highest ever seen in this class of weapon. Its design is quite conventional, a blowback weapon firing from an open bolt with a jacketed barrel, and it resembles the Bergmann MP28 *(see below)*. One unusual feature is the placing of the return spring in a tube inside the butt, connecting it to the bolt by means of a steel strut. Another was the formation of a quick-loading device for the magazine in the magazine housing. The ammunition was supplied in chargers and a suitable charger slot is cut in the upper surface

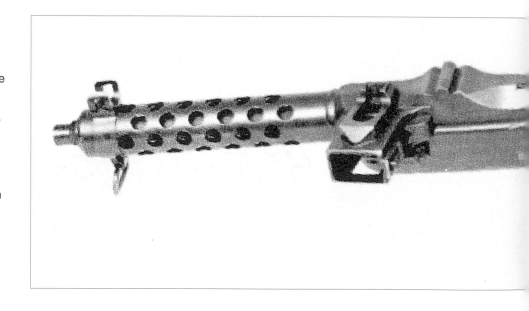

of the side magazine housing. The empty magazine slides into a secondary housing beneath this slot, the charger is placed in the top and a sweep of the thumb loads the rounds into the magazine. Once loaded, the magazine can be quickly removed from its charging position and replaced in the firing position.

Cartridge 9x19mm Parabellum
Length 33.50in (850mm)
Weight 8lb 8oz (3.87kg)
Barrel 7.75in (196mm), 6 grooves, right-hand twist
Magazine 32-round box
Muzzle velocity 1250ft/sec (381m/sec)
Cyclic rate 500rds/min
Manufacturer Steyr-Daimler-Puch AG, Steyr

The Steyr-Solothurn, showing the peculiar magazine housing with apertures top and bottom for reloading the magazine from chargers.

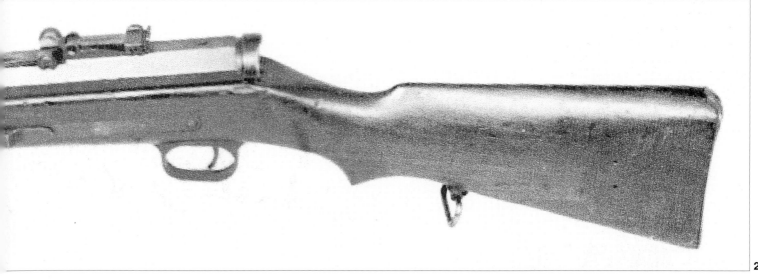

FN P90   Belgium

This unusual weapon was introduced in 1988 by FN Herstal in order to arm that two-thirds of an army whose principal activity is something other than firing a weapon – cooks, drivers, clerks, storemen and similar personnel. In addition, FN felt that the 9mm Parabellum cartridge was outmoded and so developed a new cartridge with powerful ballistic capabilities.

The P90 is a blowback weapon firing from a closed bolt. The pistol grip is well forward so that when held at the hip most of the weight lies on the forearm giving good balance and support. When fired from the shoulder the rear of the receiver acts as the butt and the curved front of the trigger guard acts as a foregrip. The receiver is largely plastic and the magazine lies on top, above the barrel, with the cartridges at 90° to the axis of the bore. A turntable device in the magazine aligns the cartridges with the bore as it feeds them down in front of the bolt. The magazine is translucent so that the ammunition content can be easily checked. Ejection is downwards, through the hollow pistol grip.

All controls are fully ambidextrous; a cocking handle is fitted on both sides and the selector/safety catch is a rotary switch beneath the trigger. There are open sights on both sides of the main collimating optical sight so that should the optical sight be damaged one set of sights can be used by either left-handed or right-handed firers.

The ballistic performance is impressive; the standard ball bullet will defeat more than forty-eight layers of Kevlar body armor at 150m range, yet the recoil force is about one-third of that produced by a 9mm Parabellum cartridge. An experimental armour-piercing discarding sabot bullet has defeated the NATO standard steel target.

By the latter 1990s the P90 was in service with fifteen countries and under evaluation by several more. There is every likelihood that the 5.7mm cartridge (which has been slightly shortened from its initial design so as to suit the Five-seveN pistol) may be confirmed as a NATO-standard cartridge and it will go into production in the USA (by Olin-Winchester) in 2000.

The P90 trigger, with safety catch, sight unit and, below the muzzle, a built-in laser projector.

Cartridge 5.7x28mm
Length 19.68in (500mm)
Weight 5lb 9oz (2.54kg)
Barrel 10.35in (263mm), 8 grooves, right-hand twist

Magazine 50-round box
Muzzle velocity 2345ft/sec (715m/sec)
Cyclic rate 900rds/min
Manufacturer FN Herstal SA, Herstal, Liege

The major component groups of the FN P90.

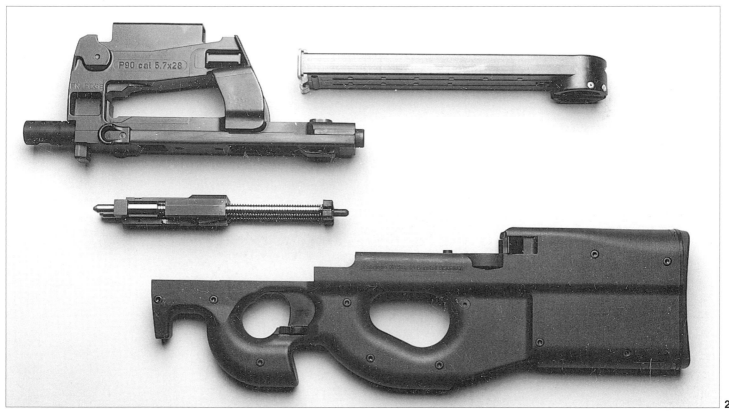

Lanchester   British

The Lanchester was made in 1941 and was nothing more than a slightly modified copy of the German MP28 *(see below)*. It was conceived in 1940 when the situation in Britain looked desperate. The MP28/II was a proven design of known reliability, so copying it made a good deal of sense. The Lanchester took its name from its designer and was made by the Sterling Armaments Company. It was originally intended for general issue, but the Sten gun *(see below)* appeared as production was beginning and the Lanchester was therefore made exclusively for the Royal Navy where it served until replaced in the early 1960s by the Sterling L2 *(see below)*. One

change from the MP28 was that the butt of the Lanchester was that of the Short Lee-Enfield Rifle; it also had a bayonet lug to take the long 1907 pattern bayonet. Other differences lay in the design of the receiver lock catch and the magazine housing: the latter component was of solid brass, fully in the naval tradition but hardly appropriate in time of war.

The magazine held fifty rounds, although the thirty-two-round Sten magazine could be inserted in some weapons. There were two versions; the original had a large Lee-Enfield rifle type of rear sight and a fire selector switch on the front portion of the trigger guard. The

later Mark I*, which was capable of automatic fire only, had a much simplified rear sight and, of course, lacked a selector switch. Most Mark I guns were later converted to Mark I* standard.

Cartridge 9x19mm Parabellum
Length 33.5in (851mm)
Weight 9lb 10oz (4.37kg)
Barrel 7.90in (200mm), 6 grooves, right-hand twist
Magazine 50-round box
Muzzle velocity 1200ft/sec (365m/sec) Cyclic rate 600rds/min
Manufacturer Sterling Armaments Co., Dagenham, Essex

The only real differences between the Bergmann MP28 and this Lanchester are that the Lanchester has a set of bayonet fittings on the front end of the barrel jacket, a prominent latch at the rear of the receiver and a slightly different sight.

The Sten took its name from the initial letters of the surnames of its designers (**Sh**epherd and **T**urpin) and **En**field the location of the Royal Small Arms Factory although much of the wartime production was subcontracted to other manufacturers, particularly the Birmingham Small Arms Company Limited (BSA) and various Royal Ordnance factories. It was a weapon born in a time of haste and extreme emergency. The threat of invasion in the summer of 1940 led to a desperate need for a light automatic weapon to arm airfield guards and antiparatroop squads, and a frantic search for a submachine gun. The Lanchester was the first solution offered, but while its production was still being organised, Shepherd and Turpin appeared in December 1940 with their 'N.O.T. 40/1' design. It was tested in January 1941, approved, Lanchester production was curtailed, and as the Sten gun it was first issued in June 1941. By 1945, nearly four million had been made in several different marks and variants.

The basic Sten was very simple and was designed so that it could be assembled from components made by small subcontractors. Cheapness and simplicity were foremost in the design and, despite some shortcomings, the Sten was one of the outstanding Allied weapons of the war; early versions cost about £2.50 to make (about $10 at 1941 rates), later ones slightly more. The Sten was never entirely popular with British troops, largely because its single feed magazine jammed frequently, though it was soon found that loading only thirty rounds reduced the problem. Another cause of jamming was holding the magazine as a front handgrip; since it was a relatively loose fit in its housing, gripping it could easily pull it to the wrong angle and cause misfeeding. Great pains were taken to train soldiers to hold the barrel jacket and allow the magazine to rest on the left forearm. When held like this, jams became much less frequent. The Sten equipped thousands of Allied soldiers, guerrillas and partisans in Occupied Europe.

The Sten Mark I consisted of a tubular receiver containing a bolt and return spring. At the front end of the receiver was a side-feeding magazine housing, a barrel surrounded by a perforated jacket and a spoon-like muzzle compensator which resisted the usual tendency to climb on automatic firing. There was a metal skeleton stock and a small folding wooden foregrip. About 100,000 Mark I and I* *(see below)* weapons were made.

Cartridge 9x19mm Parabellum
Length 35.25in (895mm)
Weight 7lb 3oz (3.30kg)
Barrel 7.75in (196mm), 6 grooves, right-hand twist
Magazine 32-round box
Muzzle velocity 1250ft/sec (381m/sec)
Cyclic rate 550rds/min
Manufacturers Royal Ordnance Factories; Royal Small Arms Factory, Enfield

The rarely seen Sten Mark 1 with front grip and muzzle compensator.

Sten Mark 1*

This was a simplified model of the Mark 1 introduced in late 1941. It did away with the flash-hider/compensator, and the wooden fore-end and handgrip which were replaced by a sheet-metal cover over the trigger mechanism.

Cartridge 9x19mm Parabellum
Length 31.25in (794mm)
Weight 7lb 0oz (3.18kg)
Barrel 7.80in (198mm), 6 grooves, right-hand twist
Magazine 32-round box
Muzzle velocity 1250ft/sec (365m/sec)
Cyclic rate 550rds/min
Manufacturers Royal Ordnance Factory, Fazackerley, Liverpool; BSA Ltd, Birmingham

Sten Mark 2

A Sten Mark 2 stripped into its principal parts, showing the simplicity of the design.

A comparison between the Sten Mark 2 (top) and a German copy made in 1945.

Introduced in 1942, the Sten Mark 2 was the most common type and the one which has usually been taken as the model for various copies. Over two million were made in three years. In general, the Mark 2 was smaller, neater and handier than the Mark 1; the barrel was a drawn steel tube held on by a screwed perforated jacket, the stock was skeletal in the extreme – generally a single strut – and the magazine housing rotated to close the feed and ejection openings when it was not in use. The gun could be easily dismantled into its component parts and so was ideal for the clandestine operations of the underground forces in Europe and elsewhere. The mechanism was simplicity itself, being little more than a bolt and spring with the most basic trigger and fire selector equipment. Sights were fixed for 100yd and they could not be adjusted for zero.

Cartridge 9x19mm Parabellum
Length 30.0in (762mm)
Weight 6lb 8oz (2.99kg)
Barrel 7.75in (196mm), 2 or 6 grooves, right-hand twist
Magazine 32-round box
Muzzle velocity 1250ft/sec (381m/sec)
Cyclic rate 550rds/min
Manufacturers Royal Ordnance Factory, Fazackerley, Liverpool; BSA Ltd, Birmingham

The Sten Mark 2S, a Mark 2 with a silencer built into it.

Sten Mark 2S

The Mark 2S differed from the standard Mark 2 in having an integral silencer, which was a long cylinder of the same diameter as the receiver and contained baffles to trap the gas. The silencer threaded on to the receiver in the same way as the normal barrel, but the barrel inside it was very short and the bullet emerged at a speed below that of sound. It was almost inaudible at a few yards, although its effective range was reduced considerably. The greatest noise came from the mechanical movement of the bolt which, in this version, was reduced in weight and fitted with a weaker return spring to compensate for the lower breech pressure resulting from the shortened barrel. The gun was intended to be fired in single shots only, as automatic fire quickly wore out the baffles and was also liable to blow off the end cap of the silencer. The life of the silencer was comparatively short, but it was an effective device and quite widely used by special forces and continued in service until after the Korean War.

Cartridge 9x19mm Parabellum
Length 35.75in (908mm)
Weight 7lb 12oz (3.56kg)
Barrel 3.50in (87mm), 6 grooves, right-hand twist
Magazine 32-round box
Muzzle velocity 1000ft/sec (305m/sec)
Cyclic rate 450rds/min
Manufacturer Royal Small Arms Factory, Enfield

Sten Mark 3

The Sten Mark 3 was the second of the series to be made in large numbers and, together with the Mark 2, was the one most frequently found in service with the British forces. It is really a variation of the basic Mark I for manufacture by alternative methods; the receiver and barrel jacket are in one piece, made from a formed sheet-steel tube which extends almost to the muzzle. The barrel is a fixture inside this jacket and so the easy dismantling of the Mark 2 is not repeated in the Mark 3. The magazine housing is also fixed. One small feature of the Mark 3 which does not appear on any others is the finger guard in front of the ejection opening – a projecting lug riveted to the receiver which prevents the firer's finger from straying into the opening. The Mark 3 first appeared in 1943 and was made until 1944, both in the UK and Canada.

Cartridge 9x19mm Parabellum
Length 30.0in (762mm)
Weight 7lb 0oz (3.22kg)
Barrel 7.75in (196mm), 6 grooves, right
Magazine 32-round box
Muzzle velocity 1250ft/sec (381m/sec)
Cyclic rate 550rds/min
Manufacturers Lines Brothers; Canadian Arsenals Ltd, Long Branch, Ontario

Sten Mark 4

The Mark 4 Sten was made only in prototype in 1943 and never saw service. It was an attempt to produce a smaller and more compact submachine gun for use by paratroops. The Mark 2 Sten was **31**

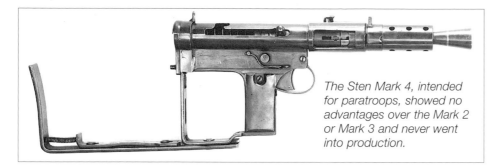

The Sten Mark 4, intended for paratroops, showed no advantages over the Mark 2 or Mark 3 and never went into production.

used as the basis. The barrel was cut until it was roughly half the original length, but it was mounted in a jacket similar to the Mark 2 and retained the same magazine housing. A flash-hider was fitted to the muzzle and a folding stock swivelled on the rear of the receiver so that it stowed forward under the gun. A catch on the stock engaged in a recess on the bottom of the pistol grip and locked it in either position. Two types were made, the differences lying in the pistol grip and trigger mechanism. Neither represented a really worthwhile improvement and it was decided not to pursue the design, the Mark 5 *(see below)* being introduced instead.

Cartridge 9x19mm Parabellum
Length *stock extended* 27.50in (698mm)
stock retracted 17.50in (443mm)
Weight 7lb 8oz (3.45kg)

Barrel 3.75in (95mm) with flash-hider, 6 grooves, right-hand twist
Magazine 32-round box
Muzzle velocity 1200ft/sec (366m/sec)
Cyclic rate 570rds/min
Manufacturer Royal Small Arms Factory, Enfield

Sten Mark 5

If the truth be told, the Sten's unpopularity was due less to the feed problems than to the undoubted fact that it looked cheap and nasty, and whenever possible some other gun was acquired and used. In 1944, an attempt was made to overcome the opposition to the Sten by producing a better version with a more robust and expensive appearance. Rather more care was taken in machining and assembly and the finish was improved, a wooden butt and pistol grip were fitted (which required the trigger mechanism to be moved forward along the receiver) and the foresight from the No. 4 rifle was adopted. This allowed the rifle bayonet

The Sten Mark 5 was made to a better degree of finish and was built to accept the standard rifle bayonet.

Mini-SAF

The Mini-SAF (1991) uses the same SIG-based construction and the same mechanism as the SAF described above but is much shorter, has no butt and has a forward handgrip which also has a guard to prevent the fingers from straying in front of the muzzle. The twenty-round magazine is the normal one, to maintain compactness, but the thirty-round magazine can be used if desired. There is a sling swivel at the rear of the receiver to which a special harness can be fitted for concealed carrying.

Cartridge 9x19mm Parabellum
Length 12.20in (310mm)
Weight 5lb 1oz (2.30kg)
Barrel 4.53in (115mm), 6 grooves, right-hand twist
Magazine 20- or 30-round box
Muzzle velocity 1214ft/sec (370m/sec)
Cyclic rate 1200rds/min
Manufacturer FAMAE: Fabricas y Maestanzas del Ejercita, Santiago

The Mini-SAF is intended for concealed carrying by security agents and use by clandestine forces.

Type 64 Silenced   China

This is a selective-fire weapon, operated by the usual blowback system and looking very much as if the inspiration for the mechanism was the Soviet PPS-43. The trigger mechanism may have been taken from the Czech ZB 26 machine-gun, though it has been simplified and is produced from steel stampings. Unlike most other silent submachine guns, the Type 64 is not a standard design with a silencer added; it was intended for one purpose from the outset and the silencer is an integral part of the design. The barrel is drilled for most of its length and fits into the Maxim-type silencer which locks to the receiver by means of a threaded ring. The receiver top is an unstressed light steel cover which lifts off to disclose the bolt and return spring and a synthetic material buffer block. There are two manual safeties; the first is a pivoting plate on the right side which swings up to close part of the ejection opening and to hold the bolt forward, much like the AK-47; and the second is a more usual button, which locks the trigger when the bolt is cocked. A change lever allows single shots or automatic fire – an unusual feature in a silenced weapon where automatic shots usually wear out the silencer very quickly. The stock folds underneath the body, and the sights have two settings marked '10' and '20' for 100m and 200m.

Cartridge 7.62mm Soviet Pistol
Length *stock extended* 33.2in (843mm)
  stock retracted 25in (635mm)
Weight 7lb 8oz (3.5kg)
Barrel 9.6in (244mm), 4 grooves, right-hand twist
Magazine 30-round curved
Muzzle velocity 980ft/sec (298m/sec)
Cyclic rate 1000rds/min
Manufacturer NORINCO, Peking

The Chinese Type 64 differs from every other silenced submachine gun in being only made in this form; all the others are converted from standard weapons.

This is an extremely lightweight weapon and a very unusual one because it is a gas-operated submachine gun and not the usual blowback. It is largely made from steel stampings and fires the usual Soviet 7.62mm pistol cartridge. The receiver is rectangular and has a safety lever and fire selector on the right side which is modeled after that on the Kalashnikov rifles. The operating system also has Kalashnikov overtones, using a short-stroke gas piston above the barrel which impels a short operating rod attached to the bolt carrier and a rotating bolt. This is a complex method of working a submachine gun but it has the advantage of resembling the contemporary rifle, so making training easier. It also does away with the need for a heavy bolt and thus makes the weapon lighter and probably rather easier to control. There are probably also manufacturing advantages and some degree of commonality of components between this and the rifle.

Cartridge 7.62mm Soviet Pistol
Length *stock extended* 29.13in (740mm) *stock retracted* 18.5in (470mm)
Weight 4lb 3oz (1.9kg)
Barrel n/a
Magazine 20-round box
Muzzle velocity 1640ft/sec (500m/sec)
Cyclic rate 650rds/min
Manufacturer NORINCO, Peking

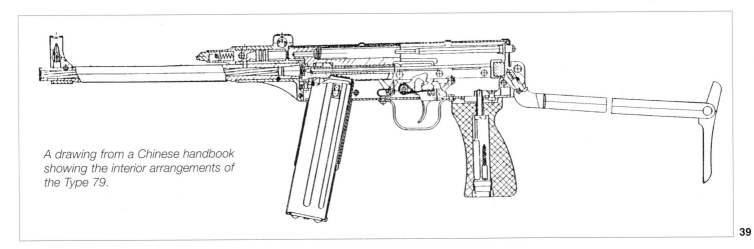

A drawing from a Chinese handbook showing the interior arrangements of the Type 79.

Type 85

China

This is a modified and much simplified version of the Type 79, a blowback weapon instead of gas operated one. The receiver is cylindrical, with the barrel screwed on at the front end, and it contains a heavy bolt and return spring. The stock folds to the right side and the magazine is the same as that of the Type 79.

Cartridge 7.62mm Soviet Pistol
Length *stock extended* 24.72in (628mm) *stock retracted* 17.18in (444mm)
Weight 4lb 3oz (1.9kg)
Barrel n/a
Magazine 30-round curved box
Muzzle velocity 1640ft/sec (500m/sec)

Cyclic rate 780rds/min
Manufacturer NORINCO, Peking

The Chinese Type 85 reverted to simple blowback operation.

Type 85 Silenced

This is a simplified and lightened successor to the Type 64 silenced weapon *(see above)*, using the Type 85 as the basis. It appears to have been developed primarily for export sales. The silencing system is the same as that of the Type 64 and although the weapon is regulated for a subsonic cartridge it is still possible to fire the standard pistol round from it, though in such case the silencer will have less effect and, of course, will only affect the report of the gun and not the noise of the bullet.

Cartridge 7.62mm Soviet Pistol subsonic
Length *stock extended* 34.2in (869mm) *stock retracted* 16in (631mm)
Weight 5lb 8oz (2.5kg)
Barrel 9.8in (249mm), 4 grooves, right-hand twist
Magazine 30-round curved box
Muzzle velocity *c.* 985ft/sec (*c.* 300m/sec)
Cyclic rate 800rds/min
Manufacturer NORINCO, Peking

The silenced version of the Type 85.

The CZ23 was designed in the late 1940s and was present in substantial numbers in the Czech Army in 1951–2, but manufacture stopped soon afterwards, when Czechoslovakia came under the Soviet thumb and was forced into line with Warsaw Pact standardisation policies. About l00,000 of these neat and handy little weapons were produced and many found their way to the Middle East and Cuba. Another model, the CZ25, was made with a folding metal stock. Both featured a bolt which had a deep recess in its forward face to allow the breech to slide inside. The bolt was about 8in (203mm) long, 6in (152mm) of which telescoped over the barrel, permitting a much shorter weapon; this is now quite common, but in 1950 it was an innovation and made the CZ23 a definite trend-setter. Another inspired idea was the combination magazine housing and pistol grip, which becomes possible when the bolt travels as far forward as it does in the 'wrap around'

method. The magazine was of the semi-triangular pattern extensively marketed by the Carl Gustav factory in Sweden and was probably the best type of magazine ever made for pistol ammunition. Two sizes were made, one holding twenty-four rounds and the other holding forty rounds.

The CZ23 and CZ25 were the first post-war submachine guns to show any significant advance in design; since then, their unique and innovative features have been widely copied.

Cartridge 9mm Parabellum
Length 27in (685mm)
Weight 6lb 13oz (3.08kg)
Barrel 11.2in (284mm), 6 grooves, right-hand twist
Magazine 24- or 40-round box
Muzzle velocity 1250ft/sec (380m/sec)
Cyclic rate 600rds/min
Manufacturer Ceskoslovenska Zbrojovka, Brno

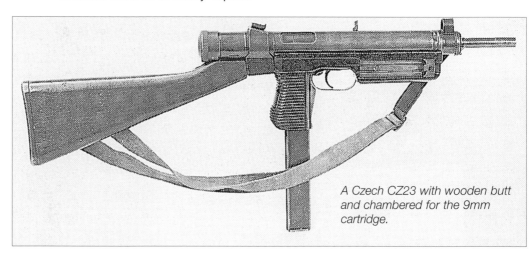

A Czech CZ23 with wooden butt and chambered for the 9mm cartridge.

The CZ24 and CZ26 replaced the earlier CZ23 and CZ25 as the standard weapons of the Czech Army when the Czechs came under Soviet domination in military affairs, and they differ from the CZ23 and CZ25 described above only in the calibre and chambering. As with all Soviet pistols and submachine guns of the immediate post-war years they fired the Soviet 7.62mm pistol cartridge. However, the Czechs have always managed to inject a little bit of difference into their 'standardisation' and in this case they loaded the cartridge to a higher velocity than did the Russians and the other Warsaw Pact armies. Apart from some obvious differences such as a new barrel, bolt and magazine, the weapon is virtually unchanged from the 9mm version. One small difference lies in the pistol grip/magazine housing which in the 7.62mm model has a noticeable forward lean, and there are some minor alterations to such items as the rear sight and sling swivels. Both the CZ24 and the CZ26 served the Czech Army from c. 1952 until the late 1960s, when submachine guns were replaced by assault rifles throughout the Warsaw Pact armies.

Cartridge 7.62mm Soviet Pistol
Length 26.6in (676mm)
Weight 7lb 4oz (3.28kg)
Barrel 11.2in (284mm), 4 grooves, right-hand twist
Magazine 32-round box
Muzzle velocity c. 1800ft/sec (c. 548m/sec)
Cyclic rate 600rds/min
Manufacturer Ceskoslovenska Zbrojovka, Brno

The CZ26 differs from the CZ23 only in having a folding butt and firing the Soviet 7.62mm pistol cartridge.

43

Skorpion vz61   Czechoslovakia

The Skorpion with the wire butt folded over the top and its diminutive 7.65mm Browning cartridge.

This is something of an oddity; chambered for the .32 Auto (7.65mm) pistol cartridge, it is closer to being a 'machine pistol' than it is to a submachine gun, and it can be holstered and fired with one hand just like a pistol. Unfolding the wire stock allows it to be fired from the shoulder, but the bullet is barely efficient enough for military use and the effective range is negligible. The object was to produce a self-defence weapon for drivers, tank crews and others who operated in confined spaces or needed something highly portable.

The Skorpion is a blowback weapon and with its light reciprocating parts a high rate of fire might be expected; the design counters this by having an inertia mechanism in the pistol grip. As the bolt recoils, it drives a weight down into the grip, against the pressure of a spring, and at the same time the bolt is held by a trip-catch in the rear position. The weight rebounds from the spring and releases the trip to allow the bolt to go forward. The duration of this action is very brief, but is sufficient to delay the bolt and thus reduce the rate of fire to manageable proportions. It might be expected that this action would make itself felt by the firer, but it is in fact masked by the general recoil and climb.

Since its original introduction, some variant models have appeared. The vz64 was chambered for 9mm Short and the vz65 for 9mm Makarov (9x18mm), but were otherwise identical with the vz61. The vz68 was chambered for the 9mm Parabellum cartridge, which made more sense, and was therefore somewhat larger and more robust. These models were primarily produced for export, but were made only in limited numbers before production ceased some time in the late 1970s.

Various models of the Skorpion went into service with Czech and Slovak army units and have been observed in use in several countries where Communist-backed rebels have been operating. It has also been manufactured under license in Yugoslavia.

Cartridge 7.65x17SR Browning
Length *stock extended* 28.95in (522mm) *stock retracted* 24.0in (270mm)
Weight 2lb 14oz (1.31kg)
Barrel 4.53in (115mm), 6 grooves right-hand twist
Magazine 10- or 20-round box
Muzzle velocity 968ft/sec (295m/sec)
Cyclic rate 700rds/min
Manufacturer Ceskoslovenska Zbrojovka, Brno

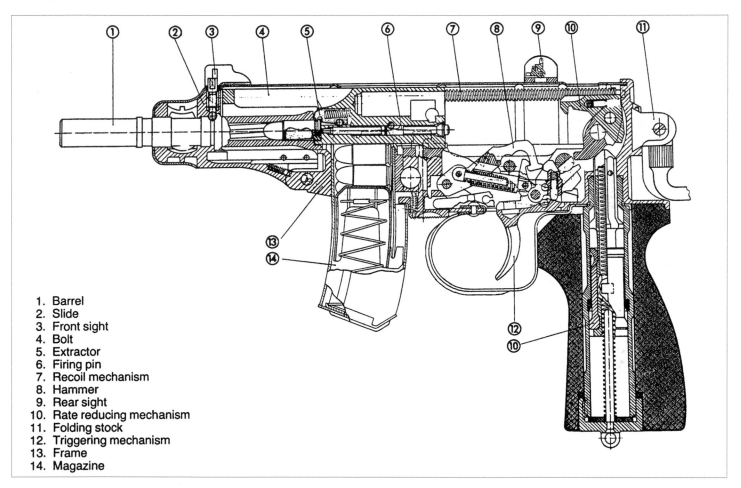

1. Barrel
2. Slide
3. Front sight
4. Bolt
5. Extractor
6. Firing pin
7. Recoil mechanism
8. Hammer
9. Rear sight
10. Rate reducing mechanism
11. Folding stock
12. Triggering mechanism
13. Frame
14. Magazine

All is revealed: the inner workings of the Skorpion; note the rebounding rate regulator in the pistol grip.

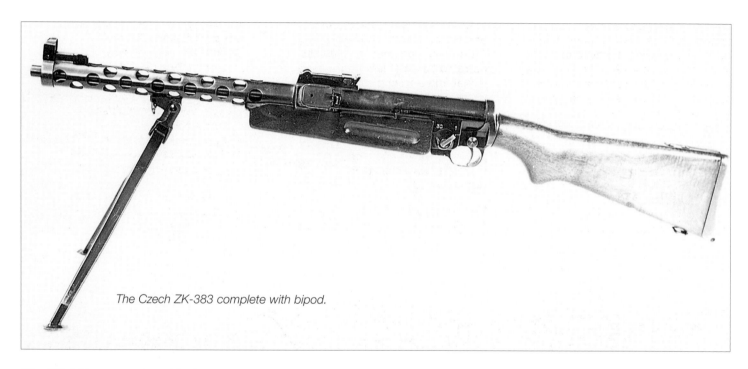

The Czech ZK-383 complete with bipod.

The ZK-383 was produced in the mid-1930s when the tactical role of the submachine gun and its place in an army were still matters for discussion. As a result it sometimes looked like a light machine gun that had lost its way, complete with bipod and quick-change barrel. At other times it was without a bipod and had a fixed barrel complete with bayonet. It would appear that the factory were prepared to make whatever adjustments they thought would attract customers and whatever adjustments any particular customer felt that he wanted. As a result it sold moderately well to Bulgaria and a number of South American states prior to 1939. During World War Two it was used by the Bulgarian and German armies, remaining in production in Brno for the latter. It stayed in manufacture until 1948, found its way to several Middle Eastern and African countries, and was still to be seen in the Balkans in the 1970s.

Basically a simple blowback design, it had one unusual feature: the bolt carried a removable weight which, when removed, lightened the bolt so as to increase the rate of fire. With the weight, it fired at 500rds/min, without it, at 700rds/min. Just how useful that feature was is open to question,

though it probably saved a useful amount of ammunition.

Early versions had a rigid fixed barrel, a bayonet lug on the barrel jacket and a front pistol grip. One variation, the ZK-383H, had a folding magazine which stowed under the barrel by pivoting on a pin, and there were police versions (the ZK-383P series) in which the bipod was discarded and a simpler rear sight was installed.

Cartridge 9x19mm Parabellum
Length 35.43in (900mm)
Weight 9lb 9oz (4.33kg)
Barrel 12.79in (325mm), 6 grooves, right-hand twist
Magazine 30-round box
Muzzle velocity 1250ft/sec (381m/sec)
Cyclic rate 500rds/min or 700rds/min
Manufacturer Ceskoslovenska Zbrojovka, Brno

The ZK-383H was intended for police use and dispensed with the bipod but had a folding magazine, seen here folded forward beneath the barrel jacket.

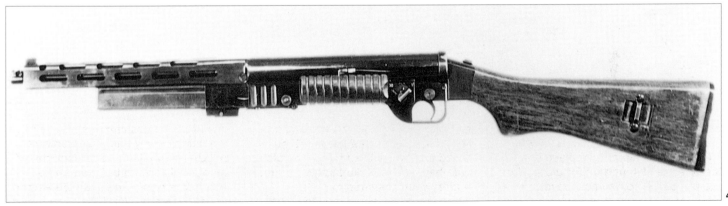

Madsen M45   Denmark

One of the last wooden-stocked submachine guns to be developed, this Madsen design dating from 1945 has some unusual features. The breechblock is attached to a slide cover (instead of a cocking handle) which extends forward over the barrel and is formed at its front into a serrated grip. The recoil spring is wrapped around the barrel and contained within this slide.

In order to cock the weapon, the slide is grasped and the entire slide and breech unit pulled to the rear – like the cocking of a giant automatic pistol. An advantage of the design is that the mass of the slide unit helps to resist the breech opening force and keep down the rate of fire, but the disadvantages are that the cover oscillates during firing, so preventing taking any sort of an accurate aim, and the spring, wrapped around the barrel and confined within the slide, soon overheats and weakens in use.

A version of the basic weapon with a folding stock was also manufactured. Like the Polish Wz-63, this is really an overgrown full-automatic pistol.

Cartridge 9x19mm Parabellum
Length *fixed stock, folding stock extended* 31.50in (800mm) *stock retracted* 21.65in (550mm)
Weight 7lb 0oz (3.15kg)
Barrel 12.40in (315mm), 4 grooves, right-hand twist
Magazine 50-round box
Muzzle velocity 1312ft/sec (400m/sec)
Cyclic rate 850rds/min
Manufacturer Madsen Rekylriffel Syndikat, Copenhagen

The Madsen M45 was built like a large automatic pistol; on firing, the entire top of the receiver came backwards, rendering the sights somewhat useless.

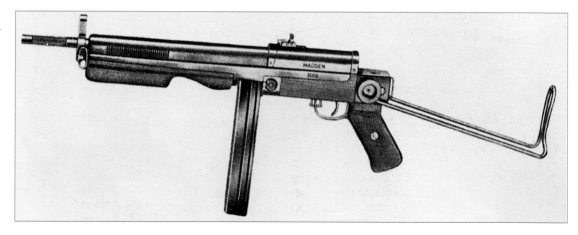

Madsen M46 Denmark

The name of Madsen had been associated with the manufacture of arms for many years and, as soon as World War Two ended, the company started to produce for the post-war market. The M46 submachine gun was an attempt in 1946 to overcome the drawbacks of the cheap and hastily made wartime guns while using their manufacturing techniques to the full. The result was a weapon which was completely conventional in operation, apart from an unusual safety catch, but which offered remarkable accessibility and ease of manufacture.

The gun fires from the normal open-bolt position and is capable only of automatic fire. A grip safety behind the magazine housing has to be grasped and pulled forward to allow the gun to fire and a second safety catch on the rear of the receiver locks the bolt in the open position. The main body of the gun is formed from two metal pressings which comprise the two halves of the entire receiver, pistol grip, magazine housing and barrel bearing; a massive barrel nut then screws on and holds both halves together. The left-hand side can be removed, leaving all the working parts in place so that internal inspection and cleaning are greatly simplified. The gun was well made and reliable, but it sold in only small numbers to a few South American countries and to Thailand. A modified pattern known as the *Maskinpistol* M50 differed in the provision

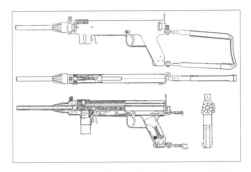

A sectioned drawing of the Madsen M46; cocking was done with the small ribbed clip riding on top of the receiver.

of an improved cocking handle which no longer had to be removed before the weapon was stripped.

Cartridge 9x19mm Parabellum
Length *stock extended* 31.50in (800mm)
  stock retracted 21.50in (546mm)
Weight 7lb 0oz (3.17kg)
Barrel 7.75in (196mm), 4 grooves, right-hand twist
Magazine 32-round box
Muzzle velocity 1250ft/sec (381m/sec)
Cyclic rate 500rds/min
Manufacturer Madsen Rekylriffel Syndikat, Copenhagen

A year went by and the Madsen M46 was a far different weapon.

The M53 is a development of the M46 *(see above)* and the M50 and differs from them mainly in the magazine which is curved to improve the feeding and can also be used as a monopod when the gun is fired in the prone position. In common with the preceding models, the receiver, pistol grip and magazine housing form a novel two-piece frame hinging at the rear, locked at the front by the barrel locking nut. An optional barrel jacket carries a bayonet attachment, which is another noticeable departure from the previous versions. Some guns have wooden furniture on the pistol grip and all have a distinctive leather sleeve on the tubular butt. Sales of this gun were fairly respectable and it was taken into service in some of the smaller countries of South America and Asia. The Madsen company left the arms manufacturing business in the 1970s, but the design has been perpetuated in Brazil.

Cartridge 9x19mm Parabellum
Length *stock extended* 31.55in (800mm) *stock retracted* 20.75in (530mm)
Weight *unloaded* 7lb 0oz (3.17kg)
Barrel 7.80in (197mm), 4 grooves, right-hand twist
Magazine 32-round detachable box
Muzzle velocity c. 1250ft/sec (c. 380m/sec)
Cyclic rate 550rds/min
Manufacturer Madsen Rekylriffe Syndikat, Copenhagen

The most ingenious part of the Madsen was the way it opened like a book for cleaning; this is an M53. When the two halves were closed, they were locked by the barrel retaining nut.

Suomi M31   Finland

The Finnish Suomi M31 seen here with a box magazine.

The Finns were among the first to realise the benefits of the submachine gun for close-range fighting in forests and they adopted a design by Aimo Lahti in 1926. Lahti then went back to his drawing board, improved a number of features and produced this M31 design, which more than one authority considers to have been the best submachine gun of the 1918–38 period. It was manufactured in Finland, Denmark, Sweden and Switzerland at various times. The 1926 design had fired the 7.63mm Mauser cartridge and had a sharply curved magazine. The 1931 pattern moved up to the 9mm Parabellum cartridge and a straight magazine or, more commonly, a drum of seventy-one rounds. Although

heavy by today's standards, it was reliable, robust and accurate and was, of course, built in the old-fashioned style, the receiver being machined from a solid block of steel. The cocking handle is at the rear of the receiver, and resembles a

rifle bolt in both appearance and initial action. The drum magazine was taken by the Soviets for their PPSh-41 gun *(see below)*. In about 1955 all the remaining M31 weapons in Finnish service were converted to accept the Swedish Carl Gustav box magazine.

Cartridge 9x19mm Parabellum
Length 36.02in (870mm)
Weight 9lb 11oz (4.60kg)
Barrel 13.58in (315mm), 6 grooves, right-hand twist
Magazine 20- or 50-round box; 40- or 71-round drum
Muzzle velocity 1312ft/sec (400m/sec)
Cyclic rate 900rds/min
Manufacturer Tikkakoski Arsenal

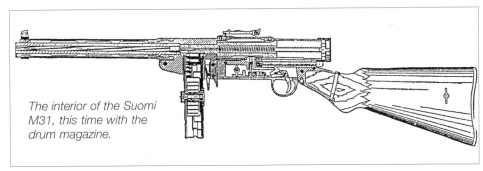

The interior of the Suomi M31, this time with the drum magazine.

A view of the Jatimatic in which the inclined plane of the bolt movement is obvious.

As is the case with modern weapons, small size and light weight were uppermost in the designer's mind when the Jatimatic was on the drawing board. And since these two desirable properties are not always compatible with accuracy and control, the weapon uses a patented design in which the bolt recoils up an inclined plane at an angle to the barrel. This causes the bolt to press against the bottom of the receiver, which tends to counter the inevitable rise of the weapon as it is fired and also gives a degree of frictional braking to the bolt. This rising path of the bolt allows the pistol grip to be set almost in line with the barrel axis and is a further element in preventing muzzle rise. There are two handgrips but no stock to this weapon, so that control is rather more difficult than normal.

The weapon consists of a pressed-steel receiver with hinged top cover. The forward folding grip beneath the barrel also acts as the cocking lever and, when closed, as a positive bolt lock. The trigger is pulled against a stop for single shots; pulling it past the stop gives automatic fire. The magazine is a double-column design and the Carl Gustav magazine will also fit. Various accessories were offered with the gun, such as a silencer, different sizes of magazine and a laser pointing device.

The Jatimatic appeared in the early 1980s, but in spite of assessment by various countries, found no takers. In

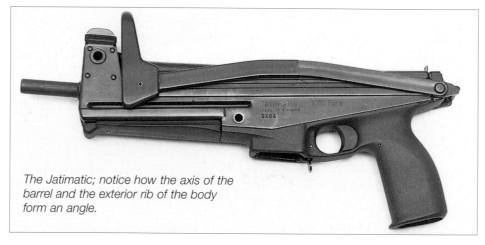

The Jatimatic; notice how the axis of the barrel and the exterior rib of the body form an angle.

the early 1990s it was offered by a Chinese company, but it rapidly disappeared again and re-appeared in Finland in the mid-1990s as the GG-95 Personal Defence Weapon, made by the Golden Gun Company.

Cartridge 9x19mm Parabellum
Length 14.76in (375mm)
Weight 4lb 5oz (1.95kg)
Barrel 8.0in (203mm), 6 grooves, right-hand twist
Magazine 20- or 40-round box

Muzzle velocity 1181ft/sec (360m/sec)
Cyclic rate 650rds/min
Manufacturer Tampeeredn Asepaja Oy, Tampere

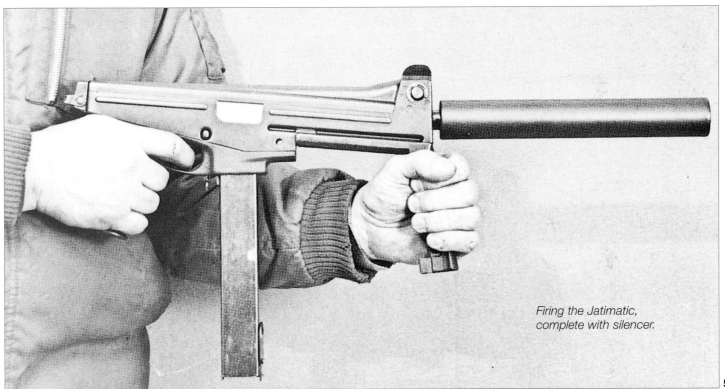

Firing the Jatimatic, complete with silencer.

French firearms design in the first half of the twentieth century was more notable for eccentricity than for any other virtue; the weapons worked, but they always exhibited some aberrant approach. In the case of the MAS 38, the bolt moves to the rear to compress a return spring buried in the butt which means that, since the butt is at an angle to the axis of the barrel, the bolt moves away at the same angle and the bolt face is therefore not square to the body of the bolt. This allows the use of a long and relatively soft spring for the return of the bolt, leading to a smooth action and a comparatively slow and controllable rate of fire. Another idiosyncratic approach was the choice of a unique cartridge, the 7.65mm *Longue,* never used by anybody else and only used in one other French weapon, the M1935 automatic pistol. It had absolutely no ballistic advantages over the more usual cartridges.

The number of these weapons produced before 1940 is not known but was probably not large. It continued in manufacture throughout the war years for supply to French police and *Milice* units, and was re-adopted by the French Army for a short time after 1945 before being scrapped in favour of the MAT 49 *(see below).* Had it been designed around the 9mm Parabellum cartridge, it might have had a longer life.

Cartridge 7.65mm *Longue*
Length 28.90in (734mm)
Weight 6lb 5oz (2.87kg)
Barrel 8.82in (224mm), 4 grooves, right-hand twist
Magazine 32-round box
Muzzle velocity 1151ft/sec (351m/sec)
Cyclic rate 600rds/min
Manufacturer Manufacture d'Armes de Saint-Etienne, Saint-Etienne

The French MAS 38 was like the Jatimatic in making the bolt move at an angle to the weapon's axis.

This might be considered as the first French design of the post-war period and the dawn of a new design era. Instead of eccentricities we find some clever design features and instead of the 7.65mm *Longue* cartridge we have the 9mm Parabellum. A simple and effective design with few frills, it is mainly made from heavy gauge steel stampings and has a minimum of machined parts, and the effort to reduce manufacturing costs has given it a very 'square' look. Nevertheless, it has survived for over fifty years and it can still be seen in the hands of the French *Gendarmerie*.

The folding wire stock is similar to that of the US M3 submachine gun *(see below)* and the pistol grip has plastic furniture and a grip safety. The magazine housing is unusual in that it pivots forward to lie under the barrel when it is necessary to carry the gun in the smallest possible package, and the housing also serves as the forward handgrip. Once the magazine is folded forward, the gun cannot, obviously, load and fire a cartridge, so the folding magazine also acts as the safety device.

The French MAT 49 was a chunky and workmanlike weapon with many ingenious features.

Cartridge 9x19mm Parabellum
Length *stock extended* 28.35in (720mm) *stock retracted* 18.11in (460mm)
Weight 7lb 11oz (3.50kg)
Barrel 8.97in (228mm), 4 grooves, right-hand twist
Magazine 20- or 32-round box
Muzzle velocity 1283ft/sec (390m/sec)
Cyclic rate 600rds/min
Manufacturer Manufacture d'Armes de Tulle, Tulle

Not many parts in the MAT 49, but a lot of clever design. **55**

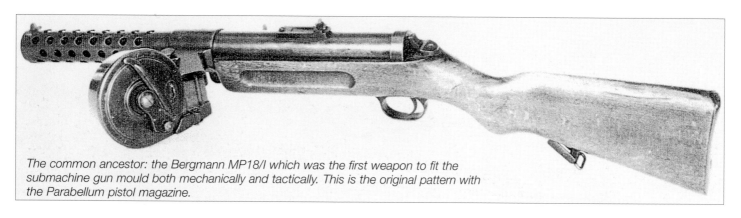

The common ancestor: the Bergmann MP18/I which was the first weapon to fit the submachine gun mould both mechanically and tactically. This is the original pattern with the Parabellum pistol magazine.

The *Maschinenpistole* 18/I was the first true submachine gun and like almost all innovative weapons it had to wait until the soldiers had worked out how to use it before it could get its start in the world. Like many Bergmann weapons it was designed by Hugo Schmeisser. It was first issued in limited numbers in 1916. As a trench weapon, it cut very little ice, but it fitted in well with the improved German Storm Troop tactics and as these were developed the MP18 found its place in battle as a means of providing massive firepower in a small package.

The MP18 consists simply of a barrel inside a perforated jacket and a receiver carrying a heavy bolt, a firing pin, a return spring and a trigger mechanism, all carried in a traditionally shaped wooden stock. The gun was originally made to use the 'snail' magazine produced for the Parabellum pistol, with which an adapter had to be used to prevent the magazine fouling the bolt; this proved unsatisfactory and was corrected after two or three years of post-war use by the police forces. A straight box magazine was substituted in the early 1920s and came in two sizes of twenty and thirty-two rounds.

The MP18 was simple, strong and reliable, and it more or less dictated the shape and form of submachine guns in Europe until the late 1930s.

Cartridge 9mm Parabellum
Length 32.10in (815mm)
Weight 9lb 3oz (4.17kg)
Barrel 7.8in (200mm), 6 grooves, right-hand twist
Magazine 32-round 'snail', 20- or 32-round box
Muzzle velocity *c.* 1250ft/sec (*c.* 380m/sec)
Cyclic rate 400rds/min
Manufacturer Bergmann Industriewerke, Gaggenau

A later version of the MP18 with a box magazine and new magazine housing.

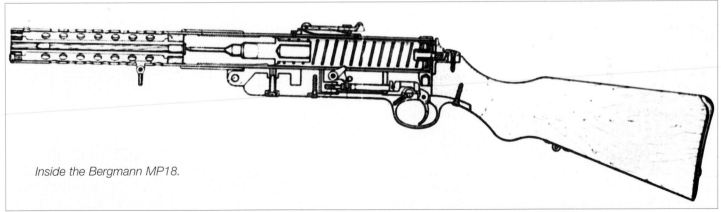

Inside the Bergmann MP18.

The MP28/II was no more than the MP18/I with a few small improvements, the principal one of which was the addition of a selector mechanism which allowed single shots to be fired. A more luxurious sight was fitted, adjustable in 100m steps to 1000m; this optimism was not uncommon in the early days of the submachine gun. There was also a new and larger return spring which raised the rate of fire. It was produced by the Bergmann company as a commercial venture, in which it succeeded, the weapon being sold to several South American countries, made under licence in Belgium for the Belgian Army, sold to Portugal in 7.65mm Parabellum calibre, and copied by various Spanish and Chinese factories. Like its predecessor, the MP28 was virtually indestructible; numbers appeared in German Army hands during World War Two, and doubtless there are several still in use in out-of-the-way places.

Cartridge 9mm Parabellum
Length 32in (813mm)
Weight 8lb 13oz (4.0kg)
Barrel 7.8in (200mm), 6 grooves, right-hand twist
Magazine 32-round box
Muzzle velocity c. 1250ft/sec (c. 380m/sec)
Cyclic rate 500rds/min
Manufacturers Th. Bergmann GmbH Berlin; Ancien Etablissements Pieper, Liege, Belgium

The Bergmann MP28 had a fire selector (above the trigger), and this one has a bayonet bar, but otherwise it was the MP18 in a new suit.

The Erma MPE followed the general pattern of the earlier Bergmanns but is instantly recognisable by the wooden foregrip.

Erma (from Erfurter Maschinenwerke) was a general engineering company in the 1920s when it was approached by a gunsmith called Vollmer; he was making small numbers of submachine guns of his own design for sale to police forces and wanted a supplier for various components. Eventually the demand for his guns outstripped his limited facilities and he sold his patents to Erma and went to work for them as Chief Designer. With a few minor changes the Vollmer gun became the *Maschinenpistole* Erma or MPE. It was manufactured as commercial venture from 1930 until 1938, when mass-production of the MP38 swept all else aside in the Erma factory. The German Army began taking deliveries in about 1933 and it remained in use until about 1942, when it was eventually withdrawn and replaced by the MP40. It was also sold in some quantities to South America.

The influence of the Bergmann can be seen in the general layout of jacketed barrel, side magazine and wooden stock. But the Vollmer-patented feature is that the firing pin and return spring are all contained in one telescoping unit, which made stripping and cleaning a simple and quick business. The main recognition point is the vertical front handgrip carved from the same piece of wood as the stock.

Cartridge 9x19mm Parabellum
Length 35.04in (890mm)
Weight 9lb 3oz (4.15kg)
Barrel 9.84in (250mm), 6 grooves, right-hand twist
Magazine 20- or 30-round box
Muzzle velocity 1250ft/sec (381m/sec)
Cyclic rate 500rds/min
Manufacturer Ermawerke B. Geipel GmbH, Erfurt

Schmeisser MK 36 Germany

When the German Army began casting about to find a submachine gun in the mid-1930s, Hugo Schmeisser got busy at the drawing board and produced the *Maschinenkarabiner 36*. In order to speed up production by utilising existing parts, he began by adopting the stock of the standard Kar 98k service rifle. Into this he then fitted a blowback action which was very similar in concept to his original MP18 *(see above)* but with one significant change: he copied the self-contained firing pin, mainspring and telescoping spring casing that had been designed by Vollmer and which was used in the Erma submachine guns. A box magazine fitted into the action from beneath the stock. The resemblance to the standard rifle was maintained by the presence of a piling hook under the muzzle and a bayonet. The sight was optimistically graduated to 1000m, though the length of its barrel meant that the weapon produced a better velocity and range than any of its contemporaries.

The weapon worked well, but the Army were not enthusiastic about it; they wanted something more compact than the standard rifle; there was little point in having a weapon of the same size. But the major objection was a legal one; he had infringed Vollmer's patents by copying the Vollmer mainspring system and under the threat of litigation he withdrew his design and abandoned it.

Cartridge 9mm Parabellum
Length 44.48in (1130mm)
Weight *unloaded* 10lb 8oz (4.76kg)
Barrel 19.68in (500mm), 6 grooves, right-hand twist
Magazine 25-round detachable box
Muzzle velocity *c.* 1350ft/sec (*c.* 412m/sec)
Cyclic rate 500rds/min
Manufacturer Th. Bergmann GmbH, Berlin

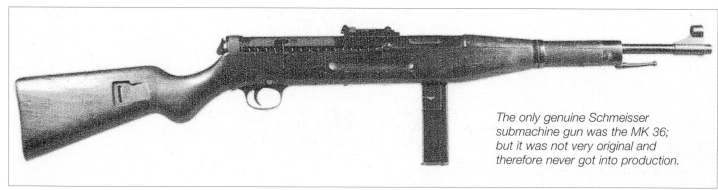

The only genuine Schmeisser submachine gun was the MK 36; but it was not very original and therefore never got into production.

The Wehrmacht's trademark, the MP38. This has a muzzle protector fitted, not a common feature. The spur beneath the barrel allows the firer to poke it through a firing port in a personnel carrier, hook the spur on the sill and fire without the weapon recoiling back inside the vehicle.

Next to the Thompson, this is probably the only other submachine gun universally recognised by the general public; and they invariably call it 'the Schmeisser'. In fact Schmeisser had nothing whatever to do with it, the weapon being designed in the Erma factory by Berthold Geipel and Heinrich Vollmer.

The MP38 was made to specifications drawn up by the German Army and from the first it was a leader in its field. It was the first submachine gun to have a successful folding stock, the first to be made entirely without any wood in its butt or furniture, and the first to be specifically intended for use by a fast moving mechanised army. The MP38 suffered, however, from two drawbacks. The first was the single-column feed system which was inefficient and led to jams, and secondly the gun was expensive and time-consuming to make owing to the large number of machining operations and the use of high-quality steel. Not long after the war started, the German authorities found that they could not afford the time and expense involved in making the MP38 and asked for a fresh design. This became the MP40 *(see below)*.

Cartridge 9mm Parabellum
Length *stock extended* 32.75in (832mm)
   stock retracted 24.80in (630mm)
Weight 9lb 0oz (4.14kg)
Barrel 9.72in (247mm), 6 grooves, right-hand twist
Magazine 32-round box
Muzzle velocity 1250ft/sec (381m/sec)
Cyclic rate 500rds/min
Manufacturer Ermawerke B. Geipel GmbH, Erfurt, and others

The MP38 cost 57 Reichsmarks to manufacture (£4.93 at the 1939 rate of exchange) which was hardly exorbitant, but it was slow to make due to an excessive amount of machining. The German Army had an insatiable demand for submachine guns and wanted faster production, so the MP40 was developed. This used stamping and welding instead of slow machining to form the parts, but was otherwise the same weapon. The price actually went up, due to the cost of new production machinery, to 60 Reichsmarks (£5.19) though this gradually came down as production proceeded and the cost of the machinery amortised. (By comparison, the standard Mauser 98k rifle was 70 Reichsmarks.) At the same time the opportunity was taken to utilise subassemblies which could be subcontracted to a host of minor firms throughout Germany. The components were then brought together for final finishing and assembly. Various small details were improved, such as the ejector and the magazine catch, matters which active service had shown to require strengthening. The result was a highly practical and effective weapon,

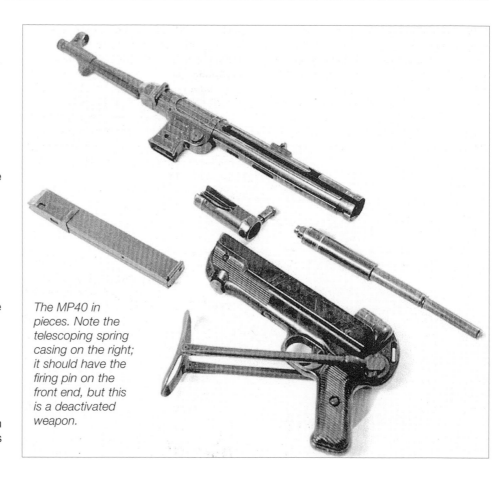

The MP40 in pieces. Note the telescoping spring casing on the right; it should have the firing pin on the front end, but this is a deactivated weapon.

Heckler & Koch MP5K   Germany

There are times when an extremely compact submachine gun is an asset – when President Reagan was shot, the number of submachine guns which appeared from under the jackets of Secret Service men was quite surprising – and the MP5K is Heckler & Koch's offering in this field. Again, it uses exactly the same mechanism as the standard MP5 but with the shortest

Covert firepower: an MP5K mounted inside a briefcase and fired by means of a trigger concealed in the handle. This case also has a laser spot projector beneath the gun and connected to the gun's trigger. (The chain is non-standard; this equipment was at an exhibition and connected to a theft alarm.)

possible barrel, short magazine, no butt and a short, rigid, fore-grip to aid in controlling it. The gun can be carried concealed under clothing or in the glove compartment of a car, or it can also be concealed in, and fired from, a specially fitted briefcase. Four versions are made; the MP5K is fitted with adjustable iron sights or a telescope if desired; the MP5KA1 has a smooth upper surface with very small iron sights so that there is little to catch in clothing or a holster in a quick draw; the MP5KA4 is the MP5K but with an additional three-round burst

facility; and the MP5KA5 is the A1 with the three-round burst facility.

MP5K
Cartridge 9mm Parabellum
Length 12.8in (325mm)
Weight 4lb 6oz (2.0kg)
Barrel 4.52in (115mm), 6 grooves, right-hand twist
Magazine 15- or 30-round curved box
Muzzle velocity 1230ft/sec (375m/sec)
Cyclic rate 900rds/min
Manufacturer Heckler & Koch GmbH, Oberndorf/Neckar

The MP5KA5 is the shortest and most compact of the MP5 family; note the symbols on the selector switch for single, three-round and automatic fire.

Heckler & Koch MP5K-PDW Germany

Defining the word 'compact': an MP5K-PDW alongside a Beretta 92 automatic pistol.

The MP5K-PDW is an MP5K with folding stock added and optional silencer.

This was developed by Heckler & Koch Inc., the company's subsidiary in the USA, as a weapon for aircrew or vehicle-borne troops who need something compact but more versatile than the MP5K. It is, in effect, the MP5K with the addition of a folding stock and with the muzzle modified to accept a silencer. There is also an interface for fitting a laser spot projector or a spotlight. If desired, the butt can be easily removed and a butt cap fitted on the end of the receiver, which more or less brings it back to the MP5K standard. Selective fire is normal, but a two- or three-round burst unit can be fitted to the trigger mechanism if required.

Cartridge 9mm Parabellum
Length *stock extended, suppresso*r fitted 31.5in (800mm) *stock retracted* 14.48in (368mm)
Weight 6lb 3oz (2.79kg)
Barrel 5.5in (140mm), 6 grooves, right-hand twist
Magazine 15- or 30-round curved box
Muzzle velocity 1230ft/sec (375m/sec)
Cyclic rate 900rds/min
Manufacturer Heckler & Koch Inc., Sterling, Ba. USA

After many years of struggling, the 10mm cartridge finally got its foot on the ladder in the early 1980s when it became the chosen FBI pistol round. It was followed by the .40 Smith & Wesson cartridge. After waiting to see whether these two newcomers would catch on, Heckler & Koch then developed two new models of the basic MP5 submachine gun to suit both cartridges.

The MP5/10 is chambered for the 10mm Auto cartridge and this has dictated the unusual forward slant of the straight magazine in order to obtain the optimum feeding angle. Apart from this there is no obvious difference between the 9mm and 10mm versions. The magazine is of carbon fibre rather than steel and there is a two-magazine clamp provided which allows two magazines to be fixed together, one in the magazine housing, allowing a very fast change.

The standard firing arrangement is the usual single shot, three-round burst and automatic selection, but any preferred combination can be provided. This weapon also marked

the introduction of the two-round burst facility, the submachine gun's equivalent of the pistol shooter's 'double tap' and which does away with the useless third round of the three-round burst, which generally went over the top of the target.

The MP5/40 is exactly the same weapon in every respect except that it is chambered for the .40 Smith & Wesson cartridge for those who prefer it to the 10mm.

Cartridge 10mm or .40 S&W
Length *fixed stock* 26.8in (680mm) *stock extended* 26.0in (660mm) *stock retracted* 19.3in (490mm)
Weight *fixed stock* 5lb 14oz (2.67kg) *folding stock* 6lb 4oz (2.85kg)
Barrel 8.86in (225mm), 6 grooves, right-hand twist
Magazine 30-round straight box
Muzzle velocity *10mm* 1450ft/sec (442m/sec)
.40 S&W 1148ft/sec (350m/sec)
Cyclic rate 800rds/min
Manufacturer Heckler & Koch GmbH, Oberndorf/Neckar

The MP5/10 is the MP5 in 10mm Auto calibre, with a two-round burst mechanism and a carbon-fibre magazine. The MP5/40 looks the same but is for the .40 S&W cartridge.

This weapon can be viewed either as a submachine gun firing a rifle cartridge or as an ultra-short assault rifle and either view would be correct. The makers call it a submachine gun and it may well be that the future of the military submachine gun lies in this direction since the growing use of body armour means that the 9mm bullet now has little chance on the battlefield except at extremely short ranges. The receiver with its wider magazine housing is that of the HK33 rifle, but the short barrel and tapering fore-end come from the MP5 submachine gun. The stock can be solid plastic or a folding two-strut metal stock, again as normal for the HK33 rifle or the MP5. The recoil impulse from the 5.56mm bullet is not particularly high and thus firing this as a submachine gun is little different to firing a 9mm weapon. It certainly has ample medium-range lethality and stopping power, making it a useful self-defence weapon. It is currently in use by a variety of special military and police forces in various countries.

Cartridge 5.56x45mm
Length *fixed stock or stock extended* 29.7in (755mm) *stock retracted* 22.1in (563mm)
Weight 6lb 12oz (3.05kg)
Barrel 8.3in (211mm), 6 grooves, right-hand twist

Magazine 25-round curved box
Muzzle velocity 2460ft/sec (750m/sec)
Cyclic rate 700rds/min
Manufacturer Heckler & Koch GmbH, Oberndorf/Neckar

Short rifle or long submachine gun? The HK53 fires the 5.56mm rifle cartridge.

Heckler & Koch HK2000   Germany

Sometimes the best intentions are frustrated by outside forces and a good design is torpedoed before it sets sail. The HK2000 is a case in point. This design appeared at an exhibition in the USA in 1991 and was a remarkable departure from Heckler & Koch's normal course. It was a blowback submachine gun and the only weapon in their military stable which did not use their roller-locked bolt delayed blowback system. The object in view was to reduce manufacturing and, therefore, sale cost and still provide a robust and reliable submachine gun. It was also designed as a 'modular' system which could be tailored to suit particular roles.

The basic weapon was a fixed-barrel blowback gun, firing from a closed bolt. It was completely ambidextrous with the safety/selector lever, butt lock, bolt catch and magazine release duplicated on each side of the receiver. There was an automatic firing pin safety system which locked the firing pin unless the trigger was correctly pulled. Perhaps the most innovative idea was a chamber gas valve which was normally closed but which could be opened to release a metered amount of propellant gas to reduce the

The shape of things to come? The HK2000 was their blowback design introduced in 1991 and almost immediately withdrawn. It is seen here with a silencer fitted.

bullet velocity to the subsonic region when firing full-power ammunition through a silencer. The barrel could be quickly removed and replaced with a barrel/silencer combination and the sights could be adjusted for use with standard or subsonic ammunition. Various sizes of magazine, front handgrips of different sorts and even a forward bolt lock for silent operation were all possible options.

The gun aroused a great deal of interest, but within weeks of its initial appearance the German government cancelled a long-standing contract with Heckler & Koch, the receivers were called

in and the HK2000 was one of a number of projects that were arbitrarily shelved to await a more propitious time.

Data for suppressed model
Cartridge 9mm Parabellum
Length *stock extended* 25.71in (835mm)
   stock retracted 14.48in (657.8mm)
Weight 6lb 3oz (3.57kg)
Barrel n/a, right-hand twist
Magazine 30-round box
Muzzle velocity 1167ft/sec (356m/sec)
Cyclic rate 880rds/min
Manufacturer Heckler & Koch GmbH,
   Oberndorf/Neckar   71

Walther MP-L and MP-K

Walther have been in the firearms business for a very long time with an impressive list of products and it is therefore surprising to find that they have only once ventured into the submachine gun field. Their design was a blowback weapon utilising steel pressings for most of its basic structure. The bolt was overhung, the bulk of it being above the barrel and overlapping the breech in the closed position, and it was located on a guide rod which also carried the return spring. The sights were an ingenious combination of open sights for snap shooting and an aperture and barleycorn for more accurate aim when time allowed.

Two models were produced, the long MP-L and short MP-K, the sole difference lying in the length of the barrel and its associated handguard. These weapons were developed in 1963 and, although excellent designs and well made and evaluated by several military authorities, they were only ever adopted by the Mexican Navy and some police forces. The prospects were not bright and in the early 1980s Walther very wisely decided to get out of this highly competitive field while they still had a whole skin.

MP-K
Cartridge 9x19mm Parabellum
Length *stock extended* 25.71in (653mm) *stock retracted* 14.48in (368mm)
Weight 6lb 3oz (2.82kg)
Barrel 6.73in (171mm), 6 grooves, right-hand twist
Magazine 32-round box
Muzzle velocity 1167ft/sec (356m/sec)
Cyclic rate 550rds/min
Manufacturer Carl Walther Waffenfabrik, Ulm a.d. Donau

MP-L
Cartridge 9x19mm Parabellum
Length *stock extended* 29.0in (737mm) *stock retracted* 17.91in (455mm)
Weight 6lb 10oz (3.0kg)
Barrel 10.12in (257mm), 6 grooves, right-hand twist
Magazine 32-round box
Muzzle velocity 1300ft/sec (396m/sec)
Cyclic rate 600rds/min
Manufacturer Carl Walther Waffenfabrik, Ulm a.d. Donau

The long and short of it: the Walther MP-L (top) and MP-K differ only in their barrel lengths.

Pal de Kiraly was a Hungarian engineer who, in 1912, patented a two-part bolt system for automatic firearms. The two parts were separated by a lever which, bearing on some fixed part of the weapon, caused the two pieces to separate comparatively slowly, thus giving a delayed opening to a blowback breech. He subsequently worked for a number of companies, developing weapons using this bolt system and in 1939 appeared in Britain with a submachine gun which, through the agency of the BSA company, he offered to the British Army. They refused it,

pointing out one or two features they did not like. Kiraly returned to Hungary, remedied the questionable features and the Hungarian Army adopted the design as the M39.

The M39 was an excellent weapon, resembling a short rifle and chambered for the 9x23mm Mauser Export cartridge. Use of this exceptionally powerful round was possible because of Kiraly's bolt system which held the breech closed until the pressure had dropped to a safe level. Another Kiraly feature was the magazine which folded up and forward to lie in a slot under the fore-end when not

in use. The muzzle accepted the standard Hungarian rifle bayonet. About 8000 of these weapons were made, most of which were lost on the Eastern Front.

Cartridge 9mm Mauser Export
Length 41.25in (1047mm)
Weight 8lb 3oz (3.72kg)
Barrel 19.65in (500mm), 6 grooves, right-hand twist
Magazine 40-round box
Muzzle velocity 1525ft/sec (464m/sec)
Cyclic rate 750rds/min
Manufacturer Danuvia Arms Factory, Budapest

The Hungarian M39 was one of the most powerful submachine guns ever made.

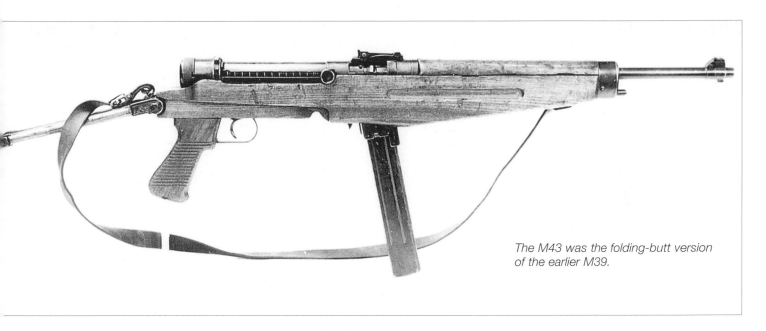

The M43 was the folding-butt version of the earlier M39.

Danuvia M43

The M43 was the M39 but with a pistol grip and a folding stock resembling that used on the German MP38 *(see above)*. The barrel was shortened and the magazine was at a noticeable forward angle, probably to improve the reliability of feeding. It served the Hungarian Army through the latter stages of World War Two and afterwards until replaced in the post-war era by Soviet weapons.

Cartridge 9mm Mauser Export
Length *stock extended* 37.5in (952mm)
  stock retracted 29.5in (750mm)
Weight 8lb 0oz (3.63kg)
Barrel 16.7in (424mm), 6 grooves, right-hand twist
Magazine 40-round box
Muzzle velocity 1450ft/sec (442m/sec)
Cyclic rate 750rds/min
Manufacturer Danuvia Arms Factory, Budapest

When Israel became an independent state in 1948, its army was equipped with an assortment of weapons, largely obsolete, collected from every corner of Europe. Standardisation on a few sound designs was a high priority and in 1949 Major Uziel Gal set about developing a submachine gun. He had already made a study of the various designs and ideas then in production and had been impressed by the compact arrangement of the Czech CZ23 series *(see above)* which used a telescoping bolt. He adopted this together with the central pistol grip which doubled as a magazine housing.

The Uzi submachine gun went into production in 1951 and has been in more or less continuous manufacture ever since. It was also manufactured under licence by FN Herstal in Belgium and was adopted very quickly by the Federal German Army. It went on to become a successful export and was adopted by many countries throughout the world for both military and police use.

The Uzi is a blowback weapon using advanced primer ignition to reduce the recoil and allow a lighter bolt. The bolt is hollow for much of its length so that at the moment of firing it encloses that part of the barrel inside the receiver.

The Uzi introduced a compact pressed-steel design with telescoped bolt and central magazine which has been in production for almost fifty years.

The firing pin is fixed so that the cap is struck and the cartridge fired a fraction of a second before the moving bolt reaches the end of its travel. Thus the cartridge explosion has to stop the bolt and reverse it before blowing it back, which reduces the recoil force and makes the weapon more comfortable to fire.

The magazine housing forms the pistol grip and the whole gun balances so well that single-handed firing is perfectly possible. There is a fire selector switch and safety catch above the pistol grip and a grip safety let into its rear edge. Early models had a wooden butt but all of the current production are fitted with a neat and strong folding stock which enables the gun to be carried by vehicle crews.

Cartridge 9x19mm Parabellum
Length *fixed stock or stock extended*
  25.60in (650mm) *stock retracted*
  18.50in (470mm)
Weight 8lb 4oz (3.75kg)
Barrel 10.23in (260mm), 4 grooves,
  right-hand twist
Magazine 25- or 32-round box
Muzzle velocity 1312ft/sec
  (400m/sec)
Cyclic rate 600rds/min
Manufacturer Israeli Military
  Industries, Ramat Ha Sharon

The more common version of the Uzi has a folding steel butt.

Simplicity itself: inside the Uzi.

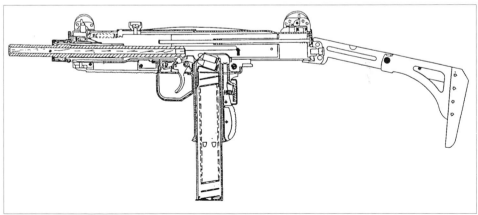

77

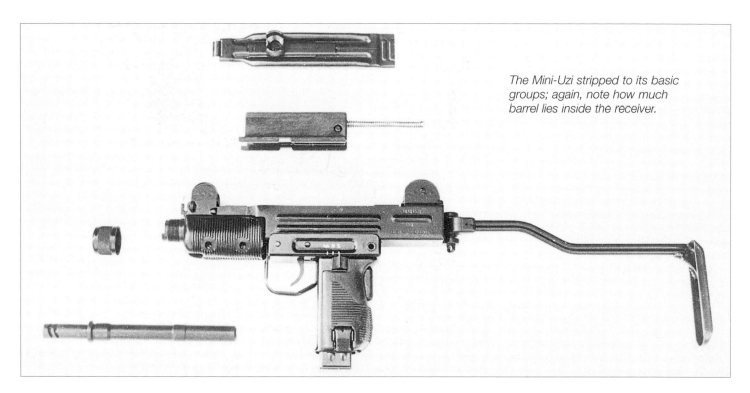

The Mini-Uzi stripped to its basic groups; again, note how much barrel lies inside the receiver.

This was developed in response to a request for a smaller weapon. In all respects it is identical with the Uzi except that it is smaller and, due to this, has different ballistic characteristics. The muzzle has compensating ports cut into its upper surface in order to assist control of the weapon. A special twenty-round magazine is provided, but it will also accept the normal twenty-five-round and thirty-two-round Uzi magazines.

Beretta Model 1918

Italy

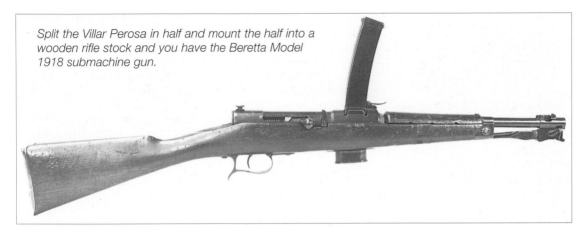

Split the Villar Perosa in half and mount the half into a wooden rifle stock and you have the Beretta Model 1918 submachine gun.

The Beretta of 1918 is a modified version of the original Villar Perosa *(see above)*. The action, receiver, feed and barrel of one half of the Villar Perosa were fitted with a new trigger mechanism and the entire unit was then fitted into a one-piece wooden butt; a folding bayonet was also provided. The resulting gun resembled a short carbine at first glance; what gave it away was the lack of a bolt handle and the short metal ejection chute underneath the stock, since, like the Villar Perosa, the magazine fitted into the top of the

action. The design was practical and useful and almost all the original V-P guns were cannibalised into Berettas.

There were two versions of the Beretta Model 1918, one with two triggers and one with a single trigger. The double-trigger version was capable of semi-automatic or full-automatic fire, depending upon which trigger you pulled. The single-trigger gun was a carbine only capable of semi-automatic fire. Both worked by a system of retarded blowback utilising two inclined planes machined in the receiver walls,

whose resistance had to be overcome before the bolt unit could rotate and move backwards to open. This slowed the rate of fire compared to the Villar Perosa which had used a similar type of retarding mechanism, but the automatic Beretta must still have been difficult to hold. Guns of this pattern were still in use in World War Two.

Cartridge 9mm Glisenti
Length 33.5in (851mm)
Weight 7lb 3oz (3.26kg)
Barrel 21.5in (318mm), 6 grooves, right-hand twist
Magazine 25-round box
Muzzle velocity c. 1250ft/sec (c. 380m/sec)
Cyclic rate 900rds/min
Manufacturer Pietri Beretta SpA, Gardione Val Trompia, Brescia

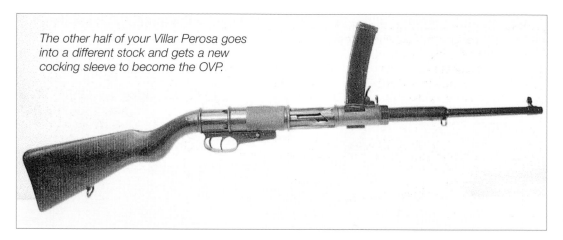

The other half of your Villar Perosa goes into a different stock and gets a new cocking sleeve to become the OVP.

When the makers of the Villar Perosa *(see above)* saw what Beretta *(see above)* had done to their brain-child, they decided that their only course was to emulate them but do a better job of it. They took their time over the design and finally produced their *Moschetto Automatico* OVP in 1920. It was adopted by the Italian Army, alongside the Beretta 1918, but by that time Beretta had taken most of the Villar Perosa guns for conversion and the Officine Villar Perosa had to be satisfied with the remainder which meant that their production was relatively small, so that OVP guns are less common the Beretta M1918s.

Like the Beretta, the OVP was half of an original V-P twin gun, but fitted with a longer barrel and a wooden butt-stock. Selective fire is possible using the two triggers; the front one gives automatic fire and the rear one gives semi-automatic fire. There was a very short fore-end in front of the trigger guard and in front of that was a prominent metal sleeve surrounding the receiver, usually left bright and with a knurled finish. This was the cocking handle. To fire the weapon, the V-P overhead magazine was inserted into the housing in front of the sleeve, then the sleeve was pulled sharply back so as to pull back the bolt and cock it. The sleeve was then pushed back to the forward position and remained still during firing.

An aperture rear sight is fitted, but it is rather too far forward, lying just in front of the magazine housing. The OVP was still in use to a small extent at the beginning of World War Two.

Cartridge 9mm Glisenti
Length 35.50in (900mm)
Weight *unloaded* 8lb 1oz (3.67kg)
Barrel 11.00in (279mm), 6 grooves, right-hand twist
Magazine 25-round box
Muzzle velocity *c.* 1250ft/sec (*c.* 38lm/sec)
Cyclic rate 900rds/min
Manufacturer Officine Villar Perosa, Villar Perosa, Turin

Beretta Model 1938A   Italy

This was the end result of a long series of development models which had begun with the Model 1918. The aim was to have a compact and reliable weapon of comparable power to the 9mm Parabellum guns and to this end a new cartridge, the M1938A, was developed which was virtually the same as, and interchangeable with, the 9mm Parabellum. The gun, though somewhat heavy, was well made and robust and went into mass production in 1938 and continued in production until 1950. It equipped the Italian Army and was also supplied to the German and Romanian armies. Early models were expensively made from machined steel and carried both a bayonet and a muzzle compensator. These refinements were dropped in the wartime versions and by 1941 a certain amount of sheet-steel had found its way into the construction and the bolt had been modified slightly. Apart from these modifications, the gun remained the same to the end of its life. As with their original Model 1918 design, the Model 1938A employed twin triggers, the forward one giving semi-automatic fire and the rear one providing fully automatic operation.

Cartridge 9mm M38A or Parabellum
Length 37.25in (946mm)
Weight 9lb 4oz (4.19kg)
Barrel 12.4in (315mm), 6 grooves, right-hand twist
Magazine 10-, 20- or 40-round box
Muzzle velocity 1378ft/sec (420m/sec)
Cyclic rate 600rds/min
Manufacturer Pietri Beretta SpA, Gardione Val Trompia, Brescia

The Beretta Model 38A had a muzzle compensator and two triggers, one for single shots and the other for automatic fire.

Although the Model 1938A remained in production throughout the war, it was expensive and difficult to manufacture in the quantities necessary in wartime and it became necessary to look for a simpler model. The Model 38/42 was a modified version incorporating a number of changes, the most noticeable of which are the shortening of the barrel and the removal of the barrel jacket. The receiver is made from sheet steel and so are several of the other parts; the wooden butt is cut square at the front and the sights, trigger guard, and other minor parts are much simplified. A new bolt handle was designed with a form of dust cover incorporated, which was undoubtedly due to the experiences of the Italian Army in the North African desert.

However, underneath all this the Model 38/42 is still the same weapon as the Model 1938A and, despite the simplifications, was still made to high standards. The rate of fire was slightly reduced and only 9mm Parabellum ammunition was used, since the difference between that and the 9mm M38A cartridge was negligible and it was found to be impracticable in wartime to issue a separate round for submachine guns. The German and Romanian armies also took delivery of this model and it may still be found either in service or in reserve stocks elsewhere.

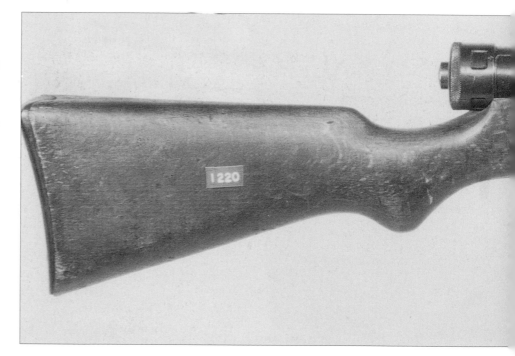

Cartridge 9mm Parabellum
Length 31.5in (800mm)
Weight 7lb 3oz (3.26kg)
Barrel 8.4in (214mm), 6 grooves,
  right-hand twist
Magazine 20- or 40-round box

Muzzle velocity *c.* 1250ft/sec
  (*c.* 380m/sec)
Cyclic rate 550rds/min
Manufacturer Pietri Beretta SpA,
  Gardione Val Trompia, Brescia

*The Beretta Model 38/42 was
simply the Model 38 design
cleaned up and simplifired for
wartime production.*

Beretta entered a completely fresh design phase with the Model 12, seen here with the metal butt folded alongside the receiver.

now had a new chief designer. It is small, compact, very well made and an early user of the idea of recessing the barrel into the bolt head. This system allows the overall length of the weapon to be much reduced without sacrificing barrel length or bolt weight. The Model 12 was designed for rapid and simple manufacture and is largely constructed of steel stampings and pressings welded together. It can be fitted with either a folding metal stock or a solid wooden one.

Cartridge 9mm Parabellum
Length *fixed stock* 26in (660mm)
 folding stock extended 25.4in
 (645mm) *stock retracted* 16.43in
 (417mm)
Weight *folding stock* 6lb 9oz (3.0kg)
 fixed stock 7lb 8oz (3.4kg)
Barrel 7.9in (200mm), 6 grooves, right-hand twist
Magazine 20-, 32- or 40-round box
Muzzle velocity *c.* 1250ft/sec
 (*c.* 380m/sec)
Cyclic rate 550rds/min
Manufacturer Pietri Beretta SpA,
 Gardione Val Trompia, Brescia

The Model 12 is a post-war design produced in the late 1950s and offered for sale in the early 1960s. It is a fresh design and owed little to the previous weapons from the same factory, reflecting the fact that Beretta

Beretta Model 12S

This is an improved Model 12, the principal changes being a new design of manual safety and fire selector and modifications to the sights. In addition, the rear cap retaining catch was strengthened and improved, a new butt-plate was fitted and the weapon was given a coating of an epoxy resin anti-corrosion finish. The Model 12S replaced the Model 12 in production in the early 1980s and became the standard for Italian forces, was sold to other armies and was also made under license by Taurus SA in Brazil. Dimensions differ slightly from those of the Model 12.

Cartridge 9mm Parabellum
Length *fixed stock* 26.0in (660mm) *folding stock extended* 26.0in (660mm) *stock retracted* 16.45in (418mm)
Weight 7lb 1oz (3.02kg)
Barrel 7.8in (200mm), 6 grooves, right-hand twist
Magazine 20, 32 or 40-round box
Muzzle velocity *c.* 1250ft/sec (*c.* 380m/sec)
Cyclic rate 550rds/min
Manufacturer Pietri Beretta SpA, Gardione Val Trompia, Brescia

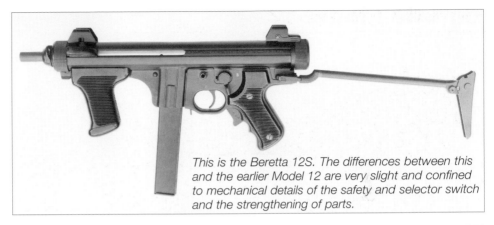

This is the Beretta 12S. The differences between this and the earlier Model 12 are very slight and confined to mechanical details of the safety and selector switch and the strengthening of parts.

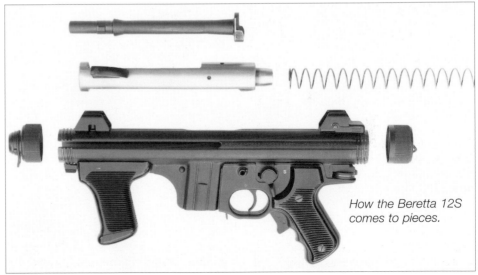

How the Beretta 12S comes to pieces.

Benelli CB-M2

This remarkable weapon was a co-operative venture by Armi Benelli and Fiocchi, the cartridge manufacturers, in an attempt to produce an entirely new weapon system which would replace conventional weapons in all calibres. The heart of the system was a 'semi-caseless' cartridge which, for those historically minded, appeared to be a reversion to the Volcanic system of the 1850s. In effect, it was a one-piece projectile consisting of a bullet and a cartridge case without a base. Propellant was packed into the open end and seated in place, while a circumferential primer ran around the propellant inside the case wall. The rounds were fed from a magazine in the normal way and the submachine gun itself was a simple blowback weapon, its only novelty being a hammer firing system which was automatically operated as the bolt closed. The bolt had a cylindrical nose which fitted neatly into the base of the cartridge and it also had seals, rather like piston rings, around its head.

As the bolt went forward it pushed a cartridge from the magazine, inserted its head into the base and rammed the round into the chamber. As the bolt closed, so the ringed portion fitted closely inside the chamber mouth, the round being held some distance inside the chamber. The hammer was then impelled on to a side-mounted firing pin which struck through a hole in the top of the chamber and thus impacted the inside priming to fire the propellant. The explosion blew the projectile off the face of the bolt and up the bore, the soft metal of the 'case' engaging in the rifling. The escape of gas to the rear was checked by the piston-rings on the bolt head interface with the chamber mouth. There was, therefore, nothing to extract and the bolt would be driven back in the usual manner to start the operating system once more.

Doing away with the extraction and ejection phase speeded up the rate of fire and the unusual construction of the cartridge allowed it to be made on conventional machinery without getting into the problems which were then (*c.* 1978) facing Heckler & Koch with their caseless G11 rifle. The manufacturers claimed that the system could adapt to any calibre, but they had elected to start with 9mm so as to have an easy comparison with contemporary weapons. Perhaps the comparison was too easy; several people examined the weapon, a number of military forces tried it out, but in the end nobody adopted it and by the end of the 1980s the CB-M2 and its AUPO cartridge were history.

Cartridge 9mm AUPO
Length *stock extended* 26.7in (660mm) *stock retracted* 16.5in (450mm)
Weight 7lb 2oz (3.40kg)
Barrel 8.1in (209mm), 6 grooves, right-hand twist
Magazine 20-, 30- or 40-round box
Muzzle velocity 1280ft/sec (390m/sec)
Cyclic rate 1200rds/min
Manufacturer Benelli Armi SpA, Urbino

The revolutionary Benelli which fired semi-caseless ammunition, an idea whose time may yet come around.

Socimi Type 821 Italy

Introduced in 1983, the Socimi design was abviously influenced by the Uzi; it uses the same layout with a telescoped bolt, the magazine feeding through the pistol grip and has a similar safety/selector switch above the pistol grip where it can be easily operated with the thumb. There are, though, some constructional differences; the receiver is a very solid rectangle into which the bolt is inserted and removed from the rear; the barrel, secured by a locking collar, can be similarly removed from the front. Most of the weapon is of light alloy, steel being used only for the barrel, bolt and various wearing surfaces. The stock folds sideways and forward to lie alongside the receiver. Accessories included a laser aiming device and a silencer.

The Type 821 went into series production and appears to have been sold principally to police forces. Production ceased in the mid-1990s.

The Socimi Type 821 with the butt and magazine removed; the layout is that of the Uzi, but the design is more rectangular.

Cartridge 9x19mm Parabellum
Length *stock extended* 23.62in (600mm) *stock retracted* 15.75in (400mm)
Weight 5lb 6oz (2.45kg)
Barrel 7.87in (200mm), 6 grooves, right-hand twist

Magazine 32-round box
Muzzle velocity 1247ft/sec (380m/sec)
Cyclic rate 600rds/min
Manufacturer Socimi Spa, Milan

90

The Socimi became popular with law enforcement agencies.

The Spectre M-4 with butt folded.

The Spectre is loaded and prepared in the normal way by inserting a magazine, pulling back the cocking handle and releasing it. This loads a cartridge and closes the bolt, but leaves the hammer cocked. Pressing a release lever now allows the hammer to go forward to be held at 'half-cock' a short distance behind the bolt. The weapon can now be carried in perfect safety. A pull on the trigger will cock the hammer then release it to fire the round in the chamber, after which the weapon acts in the normal blowback manner. Firing from a closed bolt usually means a hot barrel and a forced draught system controlled by the bolt ensures that cooling air is pumped through and around the barrel during firing. The

Introduced in 1984, this unusual weapon is the only 'double-action' submachine gun in existence. The design comes from the same root as many automatic pistol designs: a request for weapons which are safe to carry but which can be brought into action immediately without the need to operate levers or switches or to pull back slides or cocking handles.

magazines are an ingenious four-column design which compresses a fifty-round capacity in the length normally associated with thirty rounds. The Spectre has been well received and is in use by numerous security agencies.

Cartridge 9x19mm Parabellum
Length *stock extended* 22.83in (580mm) *stock retracted* 13.78in (350mm)
Weight 6lb 6oz (2.90kg)
Barrel 5.12in (130mm), 4 grooves, right-hand twist

Magazine 30- or 50-round box
Muzzle velocity 1312ft/sec (400m/sec)
Cyclic rate 850rds/min
Manufacturer Sites SpA, Turin

A long-barrelled version of the Spectre with a fifty-round four-column magazine.

Considering that the submachine gun was well suited to jungle warfare, cheaper to make and simple to operate, it is surprising that the Japanese armed forces appear to have completely ignored it. Apart from a handful of Bergmann MP28 weapons *(see above)* bought in the early 1930s, nothing was done until 1940. The design which then appeared, known as the Type 100, was obviously influenced by the Bergmann and was well made in the conventional manner by machining from the solid. It fired the weak 8mm Nambu pistol cartridge which did nothing for its performance and must have made the design difficult.

About 10,000 of the original Type 100, with perhaps another 7500 of the folding-stock parachutist's model, were made in 1941–3. The guns were not really successful, largely because little factory space could be spared for a continuous development programme and hence little effort was given to improving the weapons; another drawback lay in the poor quality of the ammunition which gave frequent jams.

In 1944, the Japanese introduced an improved model, the Type 100/44, which differed only in minor respects, but only about 8000 were produced at one of Nagoya Arsenal's subplants before the end of the war. The design of the 1944 version was much simplified to eliminate the valuable machine time which otherwise would be wasted on non-essentials.

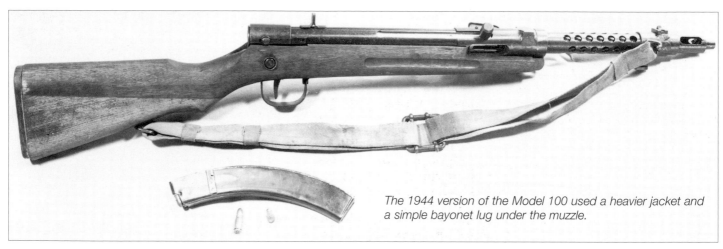

The 1944 version of the Model 100 used a heavier jacket and a simple bayonet lug under the muzzle.

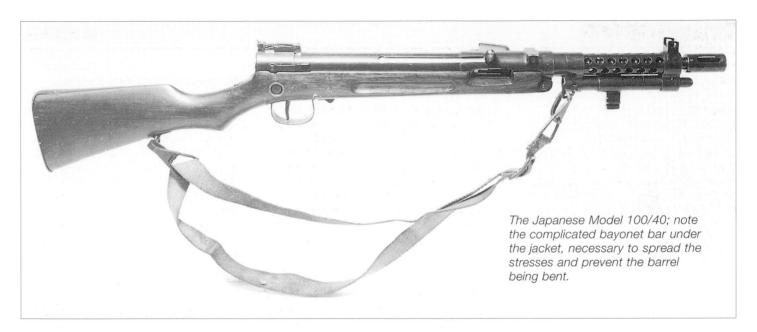

The Japanese Model 100/40; note the complicated bayonet bar under the jacket, necessary to spread the stresses and prevent the barrel being bent.

Consequently this meant the appearance of much rough welding, non-adjustable sights and a rate of fire considerably greater than that of the original 1940 version.

Cartridge 8x21mm Nambu
Length *fixed stock* 36in (914mm)
  stock extended 34in (864mm) *stock retracted* 22.25in (565mm)
Weight 7lb 8oz (3.40kg)
Barrel 9.0in (228mm), 6 grooves, right-hand twist
Magazine 30-round box
Muzzle velocity 1100ft/sec (335m/sec)
Cyclic rate 450rds/min
Manufacturer Nagoya Arsenal

Sola Super

The first ten years after World War Two saw a large number of submachine gun designs on offer as inventors tried to persuade armies to replace their wartime weapons, many of which were of poor quality due to wartime haste. The Sola was one of these aspirants and has the additional distinction of being the only firearm ever to come out of Luxembourg. It was a conventional blowback weapon capable single shots or fully automatic fire and was obviously designed with an eye to cheapness and simplicity of production, for there was considerable use of stamped components and no more than thirty-eight parts. It was, for its class, a long and cumbersome weapon, though the long barrel with an integral compensator gave a reasonable degree of accuracy and an above average velocity. But there was nothing outstanding or original on offer and this was probably why the Sola failed to gain wide acceptance. The 'Sola Super' was manufactured in small quantities in 1954–7 and marketed with some success in North Africa and South America. It was evaluated by several other countries but was never adopted by any major power.

In an attempt to make it a commercial success, the makers redesigned the weapon, doing away with the bulky trigger mechanism housing and shortening the barrel. The resulting 'Light Model' was put on the market in 1957, but met with even less success than the original 'Super'; whereupon the company decided to quit the armaments field.

Cartridge 9x19mm Parabellum
Length *stock extended* 35.0in (890mm)
stock retracted 24.0in (610mm)
Weight 6lb 6oz (2.90kg)
Barrel 12.0in (305mm), 6 grooves, right-hand twist
Magazine 32-round box
Muzzle velocity 1400ft/sec (425m/sec)
Cyclic rate 550rds/min
Manufacturer Société Luxembourgoise des Armes SA, Ettelbruck

The Sola Super, the only weapon to come from Luxembourg.

MGP-79A   Peru

Peru has a long history of purchasing weapons from outside the country, thus saving the expense of an indigenous armaments industry, but when the armed forces needed a submachine gun the Peruvian Navy decided they could do as well as any of the major manufacturers and set up Sima-Cefar as the manufacturing arm of the Peruvian Naval Base at Callao in 1979. The resulting submachine gun is a conventional blowback weapon. The barrel is enclosed in a perforated jacket; both

barrel and jacket can be easily removed and replaced with a barrel/silencer assembly. The shoulder stock folds round the right side of the receiver and the butt pad then lies alongside the magazine housing where it helps to form a forward handgrip.

The safety catch is above the pistol grip, while the fire selector is positioned close to the magazine housing, so that the two controls can be operated by different hands. The MGP-79A was the standard submachine gun of the Peruvian armed forces until

replaced by the MGP-87 in the late 1980s.

Cartridge 9x19mm Parabellum
Length *stock extended* 31.85in (809mm)
   stock retracted 21.42in (544mm)
Weight 6lb 13oz (3.09kg)
Barrel 9.33in (237mm), 12 grooves, right-hand twist
Magazine 20- or 32-round box
Muzzle velocity 1345ft/sec (410m/sec)
Cyclic rate 700rds/min
Manufacturer Sima-Cefar, Callao, Peru

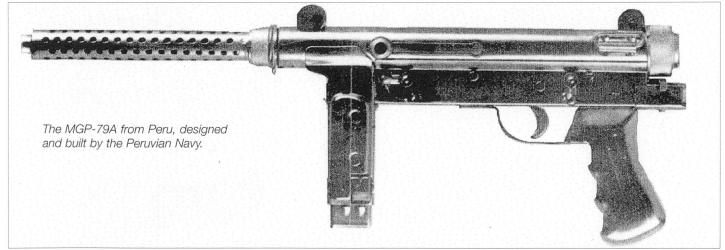

The MGP-79A from Peru, designed and built by the Peruvian Navy.

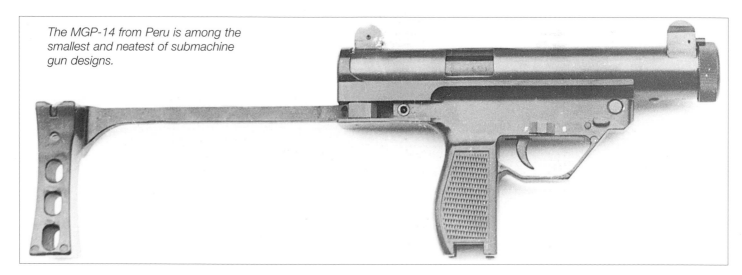

The MGP-14 from Peru is among the smallest and neatest of submachine gun designs.

This is a very small weapon designed in 1982 for use by special forces and security guards. It is a blowback weapon, the basic mechanism of which is similar to that of the MGP-79A described above. In this case, though, the barrel is considerably shortened and set back in the receiver, while the bolt is of the telescoping type, allowing the magazine to be placed in the pistol grip. The safety catch and fire selector switch is a single unit, placed ahead of the trigger guard where it can be conveniently operated by the forward hand. The stock folds sideways and the butt plate acts as a forward grip. As with all Sima-Cefar weapons, the magazine uses the Uzi interface so that Uzi magazines can be used in an emergency.

Cartridge 9x19mm Parabellum
Length *stock extended* 19.29in (490mm) *stock retracted* 10.67in (271mm)
Weight 5lb 1oz (2.31kg)
Barrel 6.0in (152mm), 12 grooves, right-hand twist
Magazine 20- or 32-round box
Muzzle velocity 1122ft/sec (342m/sec)
Cyclic rate 650rds/min
Manufacturer Sima-Cefar, Callao, Peru

The MGP-87, seen here with silencer and sling, sight adjusting tools and cleaning kit, is a simplified version of the earlier MGP-79A.

MGP-87

The MGP-87 is of the same basic design as the MGP-79A described above, but is of simplified construction: there is no barrel jacket and the barrel and the folding stock are both shorter. The cocking handle is turned up into the vertical position and made larger so that it can be readily grasped and operated. The weapon was designed in 1987 for use by counter-insurgency forces who require a more compact gun and one which can be brought into action quickly. The barrel can be quickly removed by unscrewing the securing nut and replaced by a combined barrel/suppressor unit. It replaces the MGP-79A as the standard Peruvian weapon.

Cartridge 9x19mm Parabellum
Length *stock extended* 30.16in (766mm) *stock retracted* 19.69in (500mm)
Weight 6lb 6oz (2.90kg)
Barrel 7.64in (194mm), 12 grooves, right-hand twist
Magazine 20- or 32-round box
Muzzle velocity 1187ft/sec (362m/sec)
Cyclic rate 700rds/min
Manufacturer Sima-Cefar, Callao, Peru

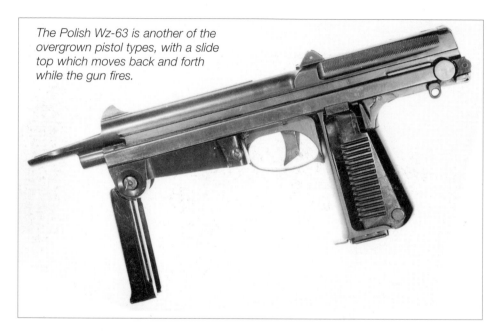

The Polish Wz-63 is another of the overgrown pistol types, with a slide top which moves back and forth while the gun fires.

Mechanically speaking, the Wz-63 is simply an overgrown automatic pistol. It consists of a frame, a slide and a barrel, just like a pistol, and even the barrel fits into the frame by interrupted lugs in the same way as the Browning 1903 pistol. The magazine fits into the butt and there is a small front grip which folds down. The butt is formed from two metal strips which slide alongside the frame so that the shoulder pad lies under the rear end. The intention was to provide a compact self-defence weapon for non-infantry troops – much the same intention which led to the Personal Defence Weapon in the late 1980s.

It is cocked by pulling back the slide until it locks. Pulling the trigger then releases it to fly forward and chamber and fire a round. The slide is then blown back and is again held, ready for the next round. Pulling the trigger harder withdraws the sear and allows automatic fire. The lightness of the slide would normally result in a very high rate of fire and therefore a rate reducer is used: this takes the form of a loose inertia pellet in the rear of the slide. After firing, the slide is held back not by the sear but by a special catch. The slide then stops moving, but the inertia pellet continues backward, compressing a spring, then rebounds forward, trips the catch and releases the slide. This device is similar to the reducer in the Czech Skorpion *(see above)* but arranged differently. The delay is in milliseconds but it serves to bring down the rate of fire to a controllable figure.

The weapon can be fired single-handed, like a pistol, or two-handed, but in either case accuracy is doubtful since the slide, and hence the sights, is moving backwards and forwards, so

The Wz-63 with magazine in place and butt extended.

This view of the Wz-63 stripped shows that it is exactly like a blowback pistol under the skin.

that aiming is impossible once the trigger has been pressed. Nevertheless, the Wz-63 is a practical enough weapon for the purpose for which it was designed in 1963.

Cartridge 9x18mm Makarov
Length *stock extended* 22.95in (583mm) *stock retracted* 13.11in (333mm)
Weight 3lb 15oz (1.80kg)
Barrel 6.0in (152mm), 6 grooves, right-hand twist
Magazine 15- or 25-round box
Muzzle velocity 1060ft/sec (323m/sec)
Cyclic rate 600rds/min
Manufacturer National Arsenal, Radom

This is said to be 'a development of the Wz-63'. In a similar way, you could say that the Boeing 747 Jumbo Jet is 'a development of the Wright Brothers' biplane': there is little or no mechanical similarity between them but the intention is the same.

The PM-84 is a much more conventional weapon, using a bolt moving inside a rectangular receiver and with the pistol grip/magazine housing located at the centre of balance (if anything, it seems to resemble the Spanish Star Z-84: *see below*). There is a sliding wire stock with a butt-plate which folds forward beneath the rear of the receiver, and a folding forward handgrip under the front end. An unusual but useful detail is the provision of two cocking handles, one on each side of the receiver.

The PM-84 is the Polish service model and fires the 9mm Makarov cartridge; a variant model is the PM-84P which is chambered for the 9mm Parabellum cartridge, presumably for export.

Cartridge 9x18mm Makarov
Length *stock extended* 22.64in (575mm) *stock retracted* 14.76in (375mm)
Weight 4lb 9oz (2.07kg)
Barrel 7.28in (185mm), 6 grooves, right-hand twist

Magazine 15- or 25-round box
Muzzle velocity 1083ft/sec (330m/sec)
Cyclic rate 600rds/min
Manufacturer Zaklady Metalowe Lucznik, Radom

The PM-84 from Poland is an entirely different weapon to its predecessor, owing more to the Uzi than it does to the Wz-63.

FBP M.48   Portugal

The FBP was a combination of the best features of the German MP40 *(see above)* and the American M3 *(see below)* guns, the design being the work of Major Gonçalves Cardoso of the Portuguese Army. The receiver section, with telescoping bolt and barrel attached by a screwed collar, was taken from the MP40, while the pistol grip, trigger mechanism and retracting wire stock were of M3 parentage. Extensive use was made of steel pressings and the result was a reliable and inexpensive weapon, though according to report, its accuracy left something to be desired.

(Right) Interior arrangements of the M.48, showing the adoption of the Vollmer telescoping spring casing.

Cartridge 9mm Parabellum
Length *stock extended* 32in (813mm)
  stock retracted 25.0in (625mm)
Weight 8lb 3oz (3.77kg)
Barrel 9.8in (250mm), 6 grooves, right-hand twist
Magazine 32-round box
Muzzle velocity 1260ft/sec (384m/sec)
Cyclic rate 500rds/min
Manufacturer Fabrica de Braco de Prata

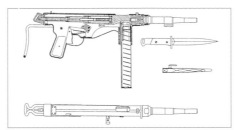

M.76

The M.76 was an improved version of the M.48 and used the same mechanical components with some modifications to improve reliability and simplify production. Two versions have been seen, one with a plain barrel and one with a perforated barrel jacket; it is probable that the jacketed model gave rather better accuracy due to giving better support for the barrel and thus removing one of the principal complaints about the M.48. Metal pressings and stampings were used for much of the construction, though the barrel was cold-swaged from high-quality steel, another factor in the improved accuracy.

Cartridge 9mm Parabellum
Length *stock extended* 31.5in (800mm)
  stock retracted 25.8in (655mm)
Weight 6lb 14oz (3.12kg)
Barrel 9.8in (250mm), 6 grooves, right-hand twist
Magazine 32- or 36-round box
Muzzle velocity 1260ft/sec (384m/sec)
Cyclic rate 650rds/min
Manufacturer Fabrica de Braco de Prata, Lisbon

From Portugal, the FBP M.48 was a local no-frills design which served for thirty years.

This became the standard Portuguese submachine gun in 1987 and is a compact and robust design owing nothing to the previous models. The receiver is in the form of a double cylinder with the barrel and bolt face In the lower section and the overhung mass of the bolt in the upper section, very similar to the Italian Franchi design. The sliding stock of steel rod retracts into the 'waist' between the two sections of the receiver. The pistol grip and trigger unit attach below the receiver and there is a prominent safety/selector switch convenient for the firer's thumb. Two versions are made, one with a detachable barrel secured by a nut, the other with a fixed barrel surrounded by a perforated jacket.

The Lusa A1 began replacing the earlier designs in the 1980s and was a much more compact weapon.

Cartridge 9mm Parabellum
Length *stock extended* 23.6in (600mm)
   stock retracted 17.5in (445mm)
Weight 5lb 8oz (2.5kg)
Barrel 6.3in (160mm), 6 grooves, right-hand twist
Magazine 30-round box
Muzzle velocity 1280ft/sec (390m/sec)
Cyclic rate 900rds/min
Manufacturer INDEP (Industrias National de Defesa do Exercito Portugues, Lisbon)

104

Lusa A2

The Lusa A2, which appeared in 1991, is an improved model of the Lusa A1. The mechanism is exactly the same, a blowback weapon with overhung bolt, and the changes are mainly in the construction of the receiver. The whole weapon is shorter and lighter, the sliding stock is stronger and slides into recesses alongside the receiver. The foregrip has been removed and the magazine and its housing now perform the function of foregrip. The barrel is retained by a screwed nut and can be removed and replaced by a combined barrel/suppressor unit, and there is provision for attaching a laser spot projector. The A2 will gradually replace the A1 as the standard issue for Portuguese troops.

Cartridge 9mm Parabellum
Length *stock extended* 23.0in (585mm)
  stock retracted 18.0in (458mm)
Weight 6lb 3oz (2.85kg)

Barrel 6.3in (160mm), 6 grooves, right-hand twist
Magazine 30-round box
Muzzle velocity 1280ft/sec (390m/sec)

Cyclic rate 900rds/min
Manufacturer INDEP (Industrias National de Defesa do Exercito Portugues, Lisbon)

The Lusa A2 is an improved version of the Lusa A1 and has now become standard in the Portuguese armed forces.

The PPD (*Pistolet Pulyemet* Degtyarev) is a general term for a series of several similar weapons produced in the Soviet Union from 1934 to 1940. The Model 34/38 was a standard issue (albeit only in small numbers) to the army until 1940 when it was supplemented by the PPD-40 *(see below)*, after which both were replaced by the PPSh-4l *(see below)*. It is a fairly conventional gun for its time, looking very similar to the German MP28/II *(see above)* and the Finnish Suomi *(see above)*. The mechanism is quite straightforward, but must have been somewhat expensive to manufacture as the components are machined from high-quality steel; there were no stampings. The twenty-five-round box magazine fed from the underside and there was also an unusual pattern of drum magazine which had a peculiar extended lip which fitted into a magazine housing in a similar fashion to a box magazine. This was the first Soviet weapon to use a drum magazine which later (though in a different pattern) became a regular feature of all but two of the entire series of Soviet submachine guns.

Degtyarev's PPD-34/38 was a workmanlike weapon but it was slow to manufacture and used a very odd type of drum magazine which was interchangeable with a conventional box.

The 7.62mm round was, of course, the standard Soviet pistol round, firing a comparatively light bullet at a high muzzle velocity. This increased velocity, however, did not give it any greater effectiveness than that of the 9mm Parabellum, nor any more range. A notable feature of this gun, and indeed of the remainder of the series, was that the barrel was chromed: an expensive process but popular with the Soviet designers as it considerably extended barrel life and resisted the somewhat cursory care and cleaning bestowed on weapons by wartime conscripts.

Cartridge 7.62x25mm Tokarev
Length 30.70in (780mm)
Weight 8lb 4oz (3.73kg)
Barrel 10.62in (270mm), 4 grooves, right-hand twist
Magazine 25-round box or 71-round drum
Muzzle velocity 1590ft/sec (485m/sec)
Cyclic rate 800rds/min
Manufacturer State Factories

After some experience with the PPD-34/38 in the Finnish forests during the Winter War, the Russians requested a few changes and Degtyarev developed this model in 1940. It was designed with a greater regard for mass production and cost. It also did away with the peculiar drum magazine of Degtyarev's design in favour of one copied from the Finnish Suomi weapon. The Degtyarev drum was designed so as to be interchangeable with a simple box magazine, but now the box magazine was abandoned and the drum and its housing could therefore be a simpler engineering proposition. The new drum was an open-top design which simply slid into the housing.

The PPD-40 was well made of good materials but it was still obviously a peacetime product; when the Russians realised the intensity of the struggle ahead of them after the German invasion and their need for masses of cheap weapons, the PPD was abandoned for weapons of even simpler construction.

Cartridge 7.62x25mm Tokarev
Length 30.60in (777mm)
Weight 8lb 2oz (3.70kg)
Barrel 10.63in (270mm), 4 grooves, right-hand twist
Magazine 71-round drum
Muzzle velocity 1590ft/sec (485m/sec)
Cyclic rate 800rds/min
Manufacturer State factories

Submachine guns armed entire formations in the Red Army; here troops parade in Moscow late in 1940 with their new PPDs.

The German invasion of 1941 cost the Russians huge quantities of equipment and much of their engineering capability, all lost in the early retreats. Manpower was low and to arm the thousands of conscripts a cheap and easily manufactured, simple weapon with ample firepower was required. The answer was the PPSh *(Pistolet Pulyemet* Shpagin) designed by Georgii Shpagin in 1941. It was

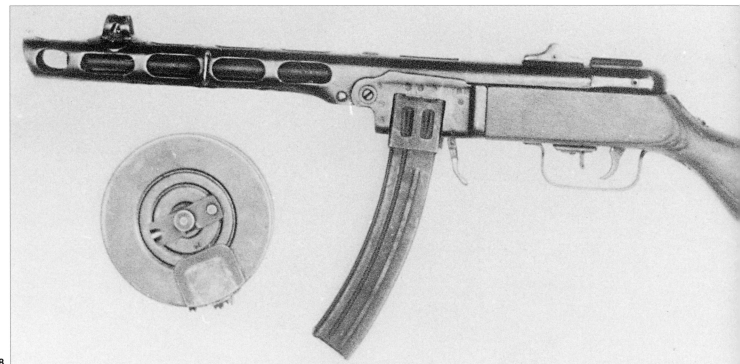

much cheaper and quicker to make than the preceding Degtyarev models and was finished roughly; the barrel was still chromed, however, and

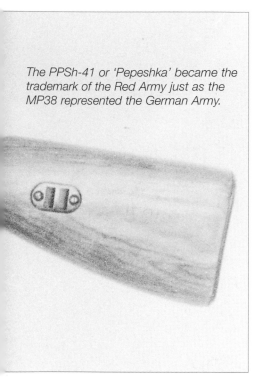

The PPSh-41 or 'Pepeshka' became the trademark of the Red Army just as the MP38 represented the German Army.

there was never any doubt about the weapon's effectiveness. Stripping was simplicity itself, as the receiver hinged open to reveal the bolt and spring. There was no selector lever on some of the late models, when the gun was capable only of automatic fire, and the magazine was the tried and proved seventy-one-round Suomi drum. The rate of fire was high, but the barrel jacket was formed into a simple compensator which helped to reduce the climb of the muzzle.

About five million PPSh guns had been made by 1945 and the Soviets adapted their infantry tactics for it; often complete battalions were armed with nothing else. It was dropped from Russian service in the late 1950s, replaced by the AK47 rifle, but it was supplied in enormous quantities to the satellite and pro-Communist countries. It was also made in various Communist countries and in Iran, and there were a multitude of minor variants.

Cartridge 7.62x25mm Tokarev
Length 33.0in (838mm)
Weight 8lb 0oz (3.64kg)
Barrel 10.50in (266mm), 4 grooves, right-hand twist
Magazine 35-round box or 71-round drum
Muzzle velocity 1590ft/sec (485m/sec)
Cyclic rate 900rds/min
Manufacturer State factories

The PPS (*Pistolet Pulyemet* Sudayev) was developed in response to a Soviet Army demand for a new submachine gun that was light, simple, made from stamped steel sheet, requiring press equipment no greater than 80 tons, and needing no more than 5 hours of machining and assembly work. No high-quality steels or alloys were to be used or any other scarce raw material. The magazine had to be quickly and easily

loaded and fitted to the weapon ' in any position and at any time of the day or year'. The design submitted by Alexsey Sudayev came closest to these requirements and was selected to become the future standard pattern on 28 July 1942.

By that time the city of Leningrad had been under siege by the German Army for some nine months, and for reasons not readily apparent, Sudayev was sent

to Leningrad with orders to bring his design into production with all speed. Since the gun design was simple, it was possible to do this using the machinery and raw material available within the siege lines, though since the German encirclement was not complete, minor but vital requirements could be met from outside. As soon as the guns were made they went into the hand of the defenders and their comments and reports led to

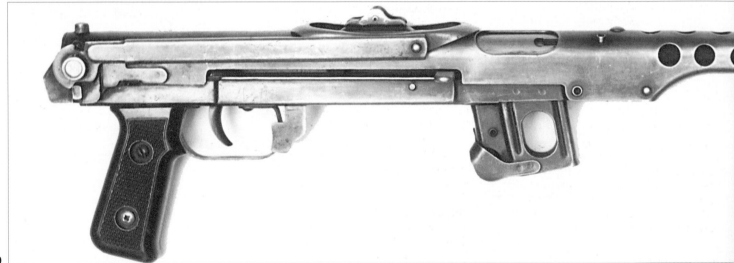

minor changes in the design before it went into mass production.

Manufacture continued after the siege was raised; it was then improved to become the PPS-43 *(see below)* which differed only in the design of the folding stock, the form of the safety catch and in the barrel jacket (which in the first model had a vertical joint in front of the magazine housing). In all, about one million of the PPS guns were made and it

The rock-bottom basic design: the only non-metallic parts are the two grips on the butt and a scrap of leather to stop the bolt hammering the back of the receiver. The PPS-43 was born in the Leningrad siege and designed around what materials and machine tools were available within the city.

continued in service for a few years after the war. It then disappeared, having been rarely offered to other Communist countries, though it was widely used by the Chinese forces in Korea in 1951–2. The Finnish M44 and M44-46 series and the Spanish/German DUX guns *(see below)* were derived from the PPS design. It is generally believed that the disappearance from service of the PPS in post-war years was due to a political decision by Stalin; the siege of Leningrad became something of a national legend of heroism and the leaders of that siege appeared to be gaining too much political influence in post-war years; they were all replaced and the gun that reminded everyone of the siege was removed from public view.

Cartridge 7.62x25mm Tokarev
Length *stock extended* 35.04in (890mm) *stock retracted* 25.0in (635mm)
Weight 6lb 9oz (2.99kg)
Barrel 10.83in (275mm), 4 grooves, right-hand twist
Magazine 35-round box
Muzzle velocity 1590ft/sec (485m/sec)
Cyclic rate 700rds/min
Manufacturer State factories

PPS-43

This was an improved model of the PPS-42. It has a shorter stock which, when folded, lies behind the ejection port. The receiver and entire jacket were stamped out of one piece of metal. It has larger protecting wings for the foresight and the safety catch is squared-off instead of rounded.

Cartridge 7.62x25mm Tokarev
Length *stock extended* 32.28in (820mm) *stock retracted* 24.60in (625mm)
Weight 7lb 8oz (3.39kg)
Barrel 10.0in (254mm), 4 grooves, right-hand twist
Magazine 35-round box
Muzzle velocity 1590ft/sec (485m/sec)
Cyclic rate 700rds/min
Manufacturer State factories

This weapon was first reported from Afghanistan late in 1983 and is a very compact version of the AKS 5.45mm assault rifle. The barrel and gas tube are much shorter and in order to reduce the violence of the gas action there is a cylindrical expansion chamber attached to the muzzle and fitted with a bell-shaped flash-hider. This also acts as a combustion chamber for any unburned powder, the usual result of firing a cartridge designed for a rifle barrel in a much shorter weapon. The receiver top is slightly different from that of the normal AK pattern, being hinged at the front end and lifting forward on opening. The steel butt-stock folds sideways and forwards to lie alongside the receiver. Some of the plastic magazines have stiffening ribs along the front rebate, suggesting that the original AKS design was not strong enough.

The Soviet entry in the small-calibre stakes was this 5.45mm AKS-74U, first seen in Afghanistan in 1982, though it had been in Soviet service for some time before that.

Cartridge 5.45x39.5mm
Length *stock extended* 28.74in (730mm) *stock retracted* 19.29in (490mm)
Weight *unloaded* 5lb 14oz (2.70kg)
Barrel 8.11in (206mm)
Magazine 30-round box

Muzzle velocity 2410ft/sec (735m/sec)
Cyclic rate 700rds/min
Manufacturer State Rifle Factory, Izhevsk

The A-91 is a good example of current trends in Russian thoughts on weapon design. It appears to be all things to all men; although offering it as a 5.45mm submachine gun, the makers hasten to point out that it can also be considered as a compact assault rifle and can be produced in virtually any calibre the customer desires up to and including 7.62x39mm.

The A-91, one of the more credible offerings from Russia; note the depth (front to back) of the magazine, necessitated by the use of a rifle cartridge.

The weapon is operated by a gas piston, tapping off the gas close to the muzzle, but the precise method of locking the breech is not stated; it is probably the familiar rotating bolt in a carrier and as far as that goes it might not be far wrong to think of this as an improved AKS-74U. However, it appears to lack the muzzle expansion chamber of the AKS-74U. These more potent rifle calibres in short barrels might prove to be something of a drawback.

There is also a variant model called the 9A-91 which is offered for the popular 'special forces' market. This is designed to fire a special low-velocity 9x39mm cartridge and is thus provided with a large sound suppressor. It can also be fitted with various other bolt-on goodies including the inevitable laser aiming spot and electro-optical sights. There are some minor mechanical changes inside the weapon due to the greater length and different characteristics of the peculiar cartridge used; it is unlikely that conversion to conventional 9mm ammunition would be possible.

Both these weapons have been seen at exhibitions in prototype form and pictures of them in use are also displayed, but as far as is known major production has not taken place and none are in service with any regular force.

Cartridge 5.45x39.5mm
Length *stock extended* 23.77in (604mm)
  stock retracted 15.11in (384mm)
Weight 4lb 5oz (1.95kg)
Barrel not disclosed
Magazine 20-round box
Muzzle velocity 2200ft/sec (670m/sec)
Cyclic rate 900rds/min
Manufacturer Institute of Precise
  Mechanical Engineering, Klimovsk **113**

The South African BXP with the butt folded under the receiver so that the shoulder pad forms a fore-end grip.

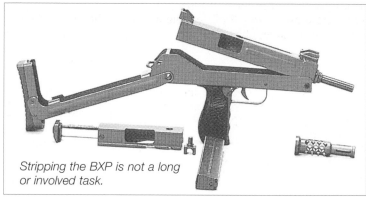

Stripping the BXP is not a long or involved task.

In the early 1950s, the South Africans equipped themselves with the Uzi submachine gun, but by the late 1970s these were wearing out and the arms boycott then in force prevented their purchasing more. Consequently, they set about developing their own design, resulting in the BXP. Made from stainless steel pressings and precision castings, it is very compact and with the stock folded can be fired one-handed like a pistol. As with the Uzi, the bolt is of the telescoped type, surrounding the rear end of the barrel when closed, but it has the additional feature that when forward it effectively seals all the apertures in the body, so preventing ingress of dirt and dust. The perforated barrel nut carries a screw-thread which will accept a compensator or a silencer which works well with standard or subsonic ammunition. There is a change lever/safety catch on both sides of the receiver and there is an extra notch on the bolt which will engage the sear should the weapon be dropped, so preventing accidental firing. The metal stock folds beneath the body with the shoulder pad acting as a forward handgrip and heat deflector. The exterior surfaces are coated with a rust-resistant finish which also acts as a life-long dry lubricant. The rate of fire is high, but the weapon is well balanced and can be controlled quite easily.

Cartridge 9mm Parabellum
Length *stock extended* 23.9in (607mm)
   stock retracted 15.24in (387mm)
Weight 5lb 12oz (2.73kg)
Barrel 8.18in (208mm), 6 grooves, right-hand twist
Magazine 22- or 32-round box
Muzzle velocity *c.* 1250ft/sec (*c.* 380m/sec)
Cyclic rate 800rds/min
Manufacturer Mechem, Silverton

Star SI-35   Spain

The Echeverria company of Eibar, who used the brand name 'Star', developed a number of submachine gun designs during the 1930s and the SI-35 is the final manifestation of all their models. The series stayed much the same in appearance and mechanism until 1942, after which the design was abandoned in favour of simpler manufacturing propositions.

The SI-35 used delayed blowback operation controlled by a locking block being driven up by the hammer (inside the bolt) to engage in the receiver body; after firing, the rearward movement of the bolt was delayed by the need to force this locking block down, out of engagement, against the pressure of the hammer and mainspring. A hold-open device indicated when the magazine was empty and, most unusual of all, a switch was provided to adjust the rate of fire to 300rds/min or 700rds/min.

While the weapon functioned reasonably well, it was unnecessarily complicated in design and difficult and expensive to manufacture. A small number appear to have been made and put into service in the closing months of the Spanish Civil War. A slightly altered version was offered to the United States Army in 1940 as the 'Atlantic' and the SI-35 was tested by the British Army at about the same time. Neither country considered the design suited to wartime production and the gun was rejected.

Cartridge 9x23mm Largo
Length 35.45in (900mm)
Weight 8lb 4oz (3.74kg)
Barrel 10.60in (270mm), 6 grooves, right-hand twist
Magazine 10-, 30- or 40-round box
Muzzle velocity 1350ft/sec (412m/sec)
Cyclic rate 300 or 700rds/min
Manufacturer Bonifacio Echeverria y Cia., Eibar

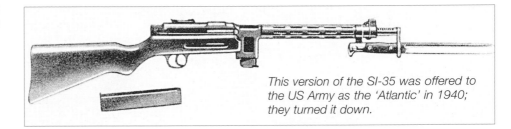

This version of the SI-35 was offered to the US Army as the 'Atlantic' in 1940; they turned it down.

The Star SI-35 appeared in various forms; this model was one of the batch offered to Britain in 1940 but turned down.

Star Z-45   Spain

The Z-45 was more or less the German MP40 *(see above)* but with a Spanish accent. It was manufactured in Spain for several years from 1944 onwards and was adopted in the late 1940s by the Spanish police and armed forces. Star had acquired copies of the original German drawings in 1942 and used these for their basic design, but then added some extra safety features such as a bolt lock to prevent accidental discharges. Selective fire was introduced, controlled by means of a two-position trigger, the initial movement of which gave semi-automatic fire and further pressure gave full automatic fire. The barrel was concealed inside a perforated jacket and retained in place by the muzzle compensator; by unscrewing the compensator it was possible to remove the barrel, a feature which, it was claimed, allowed conversion to another calibre by simply changing the barrel. The Z-45 was the first production submachine gun to use a fluted chamber, a refinement which was probably found necessary due to the higher pressures developed by the 9mm Largo cartridge.

The military version of the Z-45 was fitted with the same type of folding stock as the original MP40, but in 1945 there were still people who eyed metal stocks with suspicion, and so another version was made with a full-length wooden stock. Several South American and a few Middle Eastern countries are said to have bought the Z-45, but precise numbers are not known.

Cartridge 9x23mm Largo
Length *stock extended* 33.0in (838mm)
    stock retracted 22.80in (579mm)
Weight 8lb 8oz (3.86kg)
Barrel 7.80in (198mm), 6 grooves, right-hand twist
Magazine 30-round box
Muzzle velocity 1250ft/sec (381m/sec)
Cyclic rate 450rds/min
Manufacturer Bonifacio Echeverria y Cia., Eibar

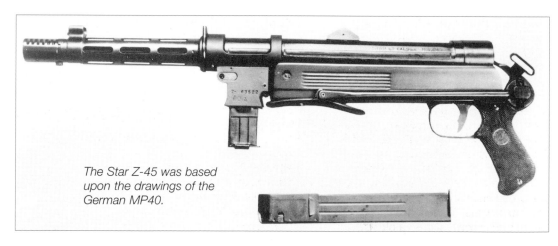

The Star Z-45 was based upon the drawings of the German MP40.

Star Z-70/B Spain

The Star Z-62 in section; the mechanism is the same in the Z-70B with the exception of the two-position trigger.

The Star Z-45 was replaced in the mid-1960s by a new model, the Z-62, which incorporated two unusual features: a hammer firing system, which was locked by the bolt except when the bolt was forward and the trigger pressed, and a double trigger which gave automatic fire when the upper portion was pressed and single shots when the lower portion was pressed. In service, it was found that this trigger mechanism gave trouble and in 1971 the Z-70/B appeared as a replacement. This uses a conventional type of trigger and a separate selector lever above the grip. The lateral push-through safety catch of the Z-62 was also discarded and replaced by a simple lever catch below the trigger guard. The rest of the design is conventional, a blowback

weapon with ventilated barrel guard and folding steel stock. It went into service with the Spanish military and para-military forces in the early 1970s and remained until replaced by the Z-84 *(see below)*.

In order to cater for the export market, a variant model of the 9mm Largo Z-62 design was made, chambered for the 9mm Parabellum round and called the Z-63. After the introduction of the Z-70/B the Z-63 model was continued in production for export sale, but was re-named the Z-70.

Cartridge 9x19mm Parabellum
Length *stock extended* 27.60in (701mm)
   stock retracted 18.90in (480mm)
Weight 6lb 5oz (2.87kg)
Barrel 7.91in (201mm), 6 grooves, right-hand twist
Magazine 20-, 30- or 40-round box
Muzzle velocity 1247ft/sec (380m/sec)
Cyclic rate 550rds/min
Manufacturer Bonifacio Echeverria y Cia., Eibar

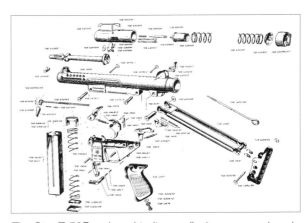

The Star Z-70B reduced to its smallest component parts.

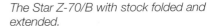

The Star Z-70/B with stock folded and extended.

A view of the Z-84 showing the clean lines and the magazine fitted into the pistol grip.

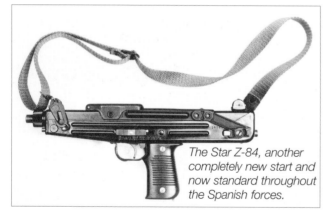

The Star Z-84, another completely new start and now standard throughout the Spanish forces.

Having taken the Z-62/Z-70 design as far as it would go, Star abandoned it and drew up an entirely new weapon, the Z-84, which entered Spanish service in 1985 and has since been sold to several other countries. In the modern manner, it uses stampings and pressings and precision castings. Particular attention has been given to the feed arrangements so that the weapon will load and fire not only the normal full metal jacket bullets but soft and hollow point and semi-jacketed rounds, a feature which makes it particularly attractive to police forces who are not under the same constraints as armies in the matter of soft-point ammunition.

The bolt is of the telescoped type, allowing the magazine to be positioned inside the grip; the bolt rides on two rails inside the receiver, giving ample clearance all round it so that there is no likelihood of its being jammed by grit or dust.

There is a sliding fire selector on the left side and the safety is a sliding button inside the trigger guard. The bolt has three notches which hold it securely in any position and there is also an automatic inertia safety unit which locks the bolt in the closed position. This is overridden by the cocking handle and is disconnected while the weapon is being fired.

As this book was being prepared for publication it was announced that the two Spanish companies, Astra-Unceta and Star (Bonifacio Echeverria), have now amalgamated to form Astar SA.

Cartridge 9x19mm Parabellum
Length *stock extended* 24.21in (615mm)
  stock retracted 16.14in (410mm)
Weight 6lb 10oz (3.0kg)
Barrel 8.46in (215mm), 6 grooves,
  right-hand twist
Magazine 25- or 30-round box
Muzzle velocity 1312ft/sec (400m/sec)
Cyclic rate 600rds/min
Manufacturer Bonifacio Echeverria y
  Cia., Eibar

closed with a live round in the hot chamber, which was not a feature that endeared itself to buyers.

So far as can be ascertained, the Rexim company never managed any worthwhile sales and the only weapons in military service were in Turkey where a number (without barrel jackets but with bayonet fittings) were issued as the 'Model 68' and remained in use until the mid 1970s. There were probably the remains of the Oviedo Arsenal stock, obtained at fire-sale prices.

Cartridge 9x19mm Parabellum
Length *stock extended* 34.35in (873mm)
    stock retracted 24.35in (617mm)
Weight 10lb 5oz (4.67kg)
Barrel 13.35in (340mm), 6 grooves, right-hand twist
Magazine 32-round box
Muzzle velocity 1400ft/sec (427m/sec)
Cyclic rate 600rds/min
Manufacturer Fabrica Nacional de Armas, La Coruña, Spain, for Rexim SA, Geneva

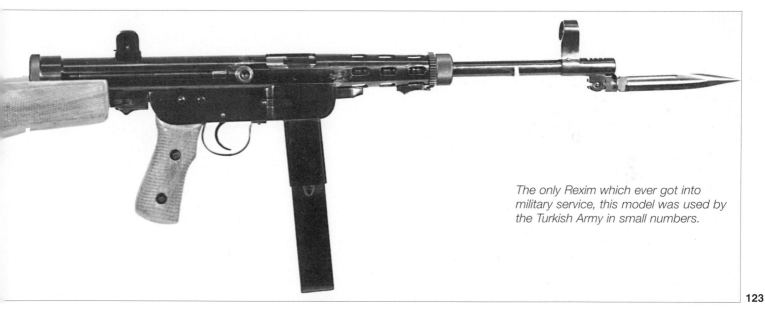

The only Rexim which ever got into military service, this model was used by the Turkish Army in small numbers.

The MP310, the final SIG venture into the submachine gun business.

SIG developed a number of submachine guns from the early 1930s onwards, but were never successful in getting them adopted by the Swiss Army and were little more successful in selling them commercially. The MP310 was their final throw in 1958 and it was an excellent weapon, conventional in being a simple and well-made blowback design but, being a SIG design, it had a few features of its own which made it just that bit different.

The magazine was a folding pattern, released by a spring-catch on the left side of the magazine housing to fold forward underneath the barrel. The trigger mechanism was constructed to give a two-stage pull, the first of which

was used to fire single shots and the second to give full automatic fire. A drum-type rear sight was used with settings for 50m, 100m, 200m and 300m. Despite the attractive features of the MP310 and the substitution by SIG of plastics and precision castings for some of their earlier weapons' expensive machined components, the gun failed to sell in large numbers; there were few buyers about in the late 1950s and plenty of war-surplus weapons available. Moreover, the Swiss government has always been magisterial about allowing the sale of arms abroad. As one Swiss manufacturer once said: 'We are only allowed to sell guns to people who don't want them.'

The MP310 was

adopted by the Swiss police and a few were sold overseas, but the lack of success seems to have decided SIG to abandon this class of weapon and they have stayed out of the submachine gun business ever since.

Cartridge 9x19mm Parabellum
Length *stock extended* 28.94in (735mm)
  stock retracted 24.01in (610mm)
Weight 7lb 9oz (3.41kg)
Barrel 7.87in (200mm), 6 grooves, right-hand twist
Magazine 40-round box
Muzzle velocity 1200ft/sec (365m/sec)
Cyclic rate 900rds/min
Manufacturer Schweizerische Industrie-Gesellschaft (SIG), Neuhausen/Rheinfalls

The MP310 with magazine folded up and butt retracted.

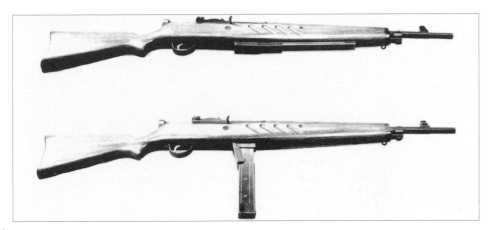

The SIG-manufactured MKMO submachine guns bear a distinct resemblance to the later Hungarian M39, doubtless due to having the same designer. This shows how the magazine folded up into a slot in the fore-end.

Pal de Kiraly, the Hungarian designer and protagonist of the two-part bolt, worked for SIG for some years in the late 1920s and early 1930s and together with the Ende brothers, also designers for SIG, developed this submachine gun in 1933. It can be seen that there is considerable external resemblance between this and the later Hungarian M39 *(see above)* and this resemblance continues under the skin since both use delayed blowback controlled by the two-part bolt. It was certainly necessary to control the breech opening since the weapon fired the potent 9mm Mauser Export cartridge. The magazine folded forward and up into a slot in the fore-end and the whole weapon was machined from the solid and built like a Swiss watch. As a result, it was expensive and failed to sell in very large numbers, though it was manufactured from 1935 until early in 1938. Most weapons were in 7.63mm or 9mm

Mauser, though the two Parabellum calibres were also made in small numbers.

A variant model was the MKPO, made for sale to police forces. This was to the same general design but had a shorter barrel and was perhaps more convenient to handle. It also had a smaller magazine and a knob-type cocking handle rather than the hook type of the MKMO.

In 1937 SIG saw that there was little future in this expensive weapon and redesigned it, doing away with Kiraly's bolt and turning the weapon into a simple blowback gun. The result was known as the MKMS and there was also a short-barrelled version, the MKPS. Neither of these produced many sales before war broke out in 1939 and shut off Switzerland from its export markets.

Cartridge 9x25mm Mauser
Length 40.35in (1025mm)
Weight 9lb 4oz (4.19kg)
Barrel 19.68in (500mm), 6 grooves, right-hand twist
Magazine 40-round box
Muzzle velocity 1640ft/sec (500m/sec)
Cyclic rate 900rds/min
Manufacturer Schweizerische Industrie-Gesellschaft (SIG), Neuhausen/Rheinfalls

125

Calico M960   USA

Remove the cover of the Calico magazine and this is what you would see. The central revolving core has a spiral rib which drives the rounds forward to the feedway.

The Calico series of weapons appeared in the early 1990s, configured as pistols, submachine guns or carbines. They all use the same system of operation, delayed blowback using a roller-locked bolt rather similar to that used in the CETME and Heckler & Koch rifles (and hence the H&K MP5 submachine gun). However, their principal feature is the ammunition supply; instead of a conventional box or drum magazine, the Calico uses a helical-feed device which allows a very large quantity of ammunition to be carried in a relatively small space, but, more importantly, allows the magazine to be placed on top of the weapon's receiver so that there are no size restrictions due to magazine housings or excessive length getting in the way.

The cylindrical magazine body carries a revolving spindle around which the 9mm cartridges are loaded and the act of loading the magazine tensions a spring. The magazine slides on to the receiver from the rear and the movement of the bolt allows the spindle to move, driven by the spring, so as to deliver the next round to the feedway. There is extensive use of light alloys and polymer materials, though the bolt and barrel are of high grade steel, and it has been said that the Model 960 with a loaded 100-round magazine weighs no more than a conventional gun with a thirty-round box magazine.

The Calico, in its various versions, was industriously promoted as a police and military weapon, but it failed to arouse much interest (except in Russia where it was soon copied) and the company closed down in 1998.

Cartridge 9mm Parabellum
Length *stock extended* 32.87in
(835mm) *stock retracted* 25.47in
(647mm)
Weight 4lb 12oz (2.17kg)
Barrel 13.0in (330mm), 6 grooves,
right-hand twist

Magazine 50- or 100-round helical
Muzzle velocity *c.* 1400ft/sec
(*c.* 427m/sec)
Cyclic rate *c.* 750rds/min
Manufacturer Calico Inc., Bakersfield,
Calif.

The Calico submachine gun with a fifty-round magazine on top of the receiver.

Colt Model RO635

This weapon, introduced in 1987, is chambered for the 9mm Parabellum cartridge but uses the basic body and configuration of the M16 rifle, with a short telescoping stock which is exceptionally rigid when extended and a blowback bolt assembly. As with the rifle, the submachine gun fires from a closed bolt and the action remains open after the last shot. The original magazine housing of the M16 remains, modified internally to take a narrower 9mm magazine. Operation and controls are the same as the M16 rifle, so that troops trained on the rifle can easily adapt to the submachine gun. It was adopted by the US Drug Enforcement Agency, law enforcement agencies and the US Marine Corps.

There are a number of variant models: the RO634 is similar to the RO635 but fires only in the semi-automatic single-shot mode. The RO639 has single-shot and three-round burst modes. The RO633HV has a barrel 7in (178mm) long, making it rather more compact, and also has an hydraulic bolt buffer to minimise the recoil forces when firing.

Cartridge 9mm Parabellum
Length *stock extended* 28.75in (730mm) *stock retracted* 25.6in (650mm)
Weight 5lb 12oz (2.59kg)
Barrel 10.50in (267mm), 6 grooves, right-hand twist
Magazine 20- or 32-round box
Muzzle velocity *c.* 1300ft/sec (*c.* 396m/sec)
Cyclic rate *c.* 900rds/min
Manufacturer Colt's Manufacturing Company Inc., Hartford, Conn.

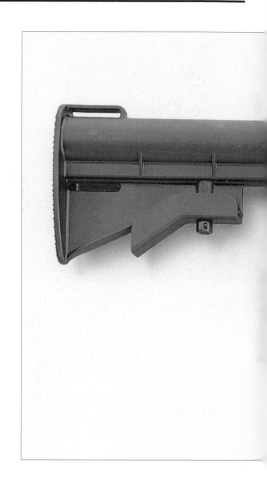

The Colt submachine gun has obvious affinities with the M16 rifle family, which makes training so much easier.

M2 (Hyde-Inland)

This was designed by George Hyde, developed at the Inland Division of General Motors and made by Marlin Firearms Corp. Often called the 'Hyde-Inland', this was another of the many weapons offered to the US Army in the early years of World War Two; at least it came from a designer of some repute, since George Hyde had already developed a gun which was used by a number of US police forces. This new design was simple and reliable and when tested in April 1942 it proved to be accurate and robust. With some small modifications, it was recommended for service adoption as the M2.

Although the M2 was a relatively simple and straightforward design, it was far from easy to manufacture, demanding some complex machining and, although the Marlin company received a contract in mid-1942, the first production models did not appear until May 1943. By that time the M3 *(see below)* had been approved for service and was in production, so manufacture of the M2 was stopped after no more than 400 had been made.

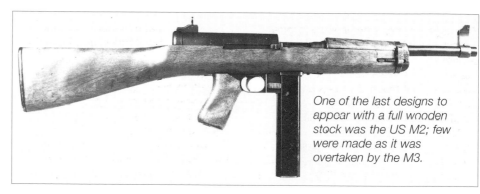

One of the last designs to appear with a full wooden stock was the US M2; few were made as it was overtaken by the M3.

The M2 was a simple blowback design, though the bolt was of peculiar shape with the rear being quite large in diameter and the front half long and slender. The receiver was built up from a seamless tubular section and a machined steel forging and it appears that the machining and finishing of this element was the Achilles heel of the design. It was a pity because the M2 shoots quite well, feels good and would probably have been a good deal more popular than the M3. One feature which is not readily apparent is that the butt, receiver and barrel are almost in a straight line, which helps to keep the muzzle down when firing from the shoulder and was no doubt responsible for the high degree of accuracy.

Cartridge .45 ACP
Length 32.1in (825mm)
Weight 9lb 4oz (4.19kg)
Barrel 12.1in (307mm), 4 grooves, right-hand twist
Magazine 20 or 30-round Thompson box
Muzzle velocity 960ft/sec (293m/sec)
Cyclic rate 500rds/min
Manufacturer Marlin Firearms Corp., New Haven, Conn.

Ingram Model 6

The Ingram is not a particularly inspired design, but it is one of the very few which reached any sort of quantity production in the United States in the years after World War Two. The Model 6 appeared in the early 1950s and was sold in limited numbers to various police forces, the Cuban Navy, the Peruvian Army and the Thailand forces. Like so many American designs of the 1930–50 period, it followed closely on the lines of the Thompson, with its front pistol grip and tapering barrel. A simple blowback weapon, its only unusual feature (for an American design) was the use of a two-stage trigger to provide single shots or automatic fire. Ingram took considerable pains to produce a design which could be made by any competent machine shop from simple tubing and strip metal; there was very little machining involved and no requirement for expensive stamping presses. It was hoped that this would make it attractive to smaller countries wishing to manufacture their own weapons. But at that time there was little or no requirement for such a weapon on the American continent and the rest of the world was awash with cheap war-surplus weapons. Ingram was lucky to find any market at all.

Cartridge .45 ACP
Length 30.0in (762mm)
Weight 7lb 4oz (3.29kg)
Barrel 9.0in (228mm), 6 grooves, right-hand twist
Magazine 30-round box
Muzzle velocity 920ft/sec (280m/sec)
Cyclic rate 600rds/min
Manufacturer Police Ordnance Corp., Los Angeles, Calif.

The Ingram Model 6 echoed the shape of the Thompson, a common feature of American designs of the 1940s.

Ingram Model 10

Gordon Ingram left the Police Ordnance Corporation and in 1970 developed this submachine gun for the Military Armament Corporation. The Model 10 was extremely compact and built of steel pressings and there seems little doubt that it tried to emulate the features of the Uzi but in a more utilitarian package. The bolt was of the 'overhung' or telescoping type, enveloping the rear end of the barrel when closed, and the magazine fed through the pistol grip; these two features ensured that the centre of balance was over the grip, which gave a very steady weapon and even allowed it to be fired with one hand. A cocking handle protruded through the top of the receiver and was notched to allow an uninterrupted line of sight; to lock the bolt, this handle was rotated through 90° and this, of course, obstructed the sight line and acted as an indication that the weapon was locked in a safe condition.

The barrel of the Ingram was threaded to accept a 'sound suppressor'; this was similar to a silencer but only muffled the sound of

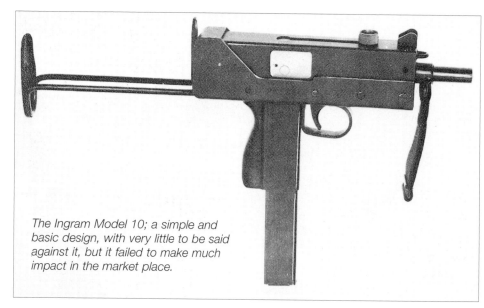

The Ingram Model 10; a simple and basic design, with very little to be said against it, but it failed to make much impact in the market place.

discharge and made no attempt to reduce the velocity of the bullet. Small quantities of the Model 10 were sold to several countries, but the company was undercapitalised and went into liquidation. The design then passed through the hands of several other firms who attempted to promote the weapon with little success until production finally ceased some time in the mid-1980s. The Ingram received enormous publicity and was prominently seen in several films and TV series, but in real life it failed to achieve the success it was thought to deserve.

The immortal Thompson, the weapon which introduced the words 'submachine gun' to the world. This is the M1928 model as originally issued to the US Marines.

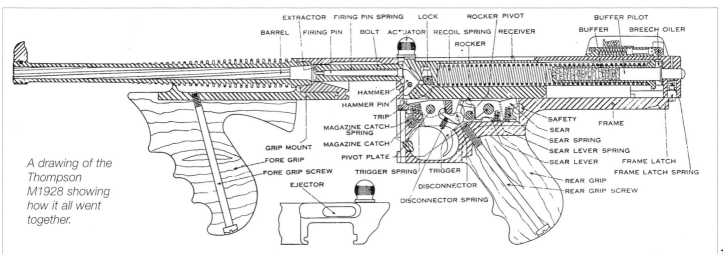

A drawing of the Thompson M1928 showing how it all went together.

EXTRACTOR FIRING PIN SPRING LOCK ROCKER PIVOT BUFFER PILOT

BARREL FIRING PIN BOLT ACTUATOR RECOIL SPRING RECEIVER BUFFER BREECH OILER

ROCKER

HAMMER

HAMMER PIN

TRIP SAFETY FRAME

MAGAZINE CATCH SPRING SEAR

MAGAZINE CATCH SEAR SPRING

GRIP MOUNT PIVOT PLATE SEAR LEVER SPRING

FORE GRIP SEAR LEVER FRAME LATCH

FORE GRIP SCREW TRIGGER SPRING TRIGGER FRAME LATCH SPRING

EJECTOR DISCONNECTOR REAR GRIP

DISCONNECTOR SPRING REAR GRIP SCREW

Thompson M1

The demand for the Thompson submachine gun increased overnight on the outbreak of war in 1939 and took another upwards leap when the USA entered in 1941. The gun went back into production and it was soon found that the design was not well suited to mass production. By 1942, it became imperative to simplify the weapon in order to keep up the supplies. The Savage Arms Corporation, who were manufacturing the M1928 gun, modified the design by removing the Blish bolt locking system and the result was the M1, a simple blowback weapon rather than the delayed blowback gun of the original models. The bolt was slightly heavier, the cocking handle was moved to the right-hand side and the sights were considerably simplified. The drum magazine was dropped in favor of the twenty- and thirty-round boxes, the muzzle compensator disappeared and the vertical front handgrip was replaced by a more conventional horizontal fore-end. The M1A1 further simplified the design by introducing a fixed firing pin in place of the original hammer.

The Thompson in all its various forms was a popular gun and was always preferred to the Sten and the M3. It continued in production until 1945, reappeared in the Korean War and was still being offered to Asian countries under the Offshore Program as late as 1960. It is no longer in service with any major military force, but the guns were so well made that they will last for a good many years yet.

Cartridge .45 ACP
Length 32.0in (813mm)
Weight 10lb 7oz (4.74kg)
Barrel 10.50in (198mm), 6 grooves, right-hand twist
Magazine 20- or 30-round box
Muzzle velocity 920ft/sec (280m/sec)
Cyclic rate 700rds/min
Manufacturers Auto-Ordnance Corp., West Hurley, NY; Savage Arms Corp., Utica, NY

To speed up wartime production, the Thompson M1 appeared, with the delayed blowback components removed and the cocking handle moved to the side of the receiver.

United Defense UD M42 USA

The United Defense UD M42 which was sold to the Dutch in some quantity. An interesting point here is the up-and-down double magazine, a trick frequently done with sticky tape but rarely provided as a manufactured item.

The United Defense UD M42 was designed in the late 1930s by Carl Swebilius of the High Standard Corporation, but manufacture did not begin until late 1941 when some 15,000 were made by the Marlin Firearms Corporation for the United Defense Supply Corporation, a purchasing agency set up by the US Government to channel weapons to various overseas buyers. A large number of these weapons were supplied to the Dutch Purchasing Commission for delivery to the Netherlands East Indies Army, but the rapid movement of the Japanese soon put that destination out of business and the balance of the production appears to have been supplied to the

Office of Strategic Services for use by clandestine organisations.

The UD M42 was rather more complicated than the usual blowback weapon, using a bolt which incorporated a trip hammer and a loose firing pin held back by a spring. It fired from an open bolt and as the bolt closed, the hammer was caught by a lug in the receiver and rotated so as to strike the firing pin. It was also unusual in having a hold-open device which held the bolt to the rear after the last shot in the magazine had been fired; the magazine could then be changed and the insertion of the fresh magazine released the bolt stop and allowed the bolt to be held on the sear, ready to resume firing without having, as

in most submachine guns, to pull back the cocking handle.

A .45in version was made, but it was unfortunate in appearing just after the Thompson had got into full production, so that it never gained a military contract.

Cartridge 9x19mm Parabellum
Length 32.25n (820mm)
Weight 9lb 1oz (4.17kg)
Barrel 11.0in (279mm), 6 grooves, right-hand twist
Magazine 20-round box
Muzzle velocity 1312ft/sec (400m/sec)
Cyclic rate 700rds/min
Manufacturer Marlin Firearms Corp., New Haven, Conn.

When the United States entered World War Two, the US Army immediately began searching for a replacement for the expensive and difficult Thompson. There was no shortage of designs, which rained upon them from all directions, and some of the inventors actually had working guns to demonstrate. But all of them were 'traditional' designs, using expensive and slowly machined components, expensively finished and with polished wooden furniture, and the Army found it almost impossible to make the designers think of abandoning this for something cheap and quick. The only solution, it seemed, was for the Army itself to design the thing and a team was assembled at Aberdeen Proving Ground, given a Sten gun as an example of the sort of thing that was wanted and told to get on with it. Even they found it difficult to overcome the traditional ideas, but within two years a new design was in production.

This was the M3 – a simple, robust, cheap and entirely adequate gun which apparently fulfilled the specification in

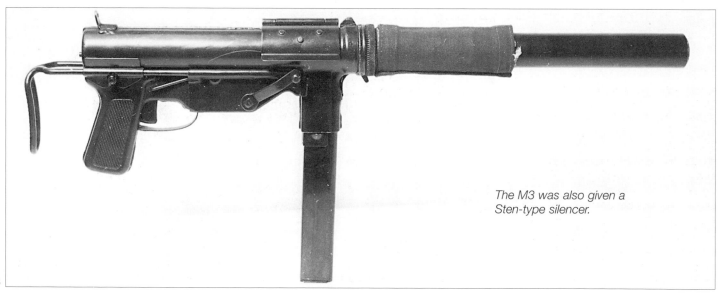

The M3 was also given a Sten-type silencer.

COMPARATIVE TABLE OF SUBMACHINE GUNS

Name	Year	Calibre (mm)	Action	Overall length (in)	Barrel length (in)	Weight	Magazine capacity	Muzzle velocity (ft/sec)	Cyclic rate (rds/min)
5.45mm Soviet									
A-91	1995	5.45x39	Gas	23.77	n/a	4lb 5oz	20	2200	900
AKS-74U	1980	5.45x39	Gas	28.74	8.11	5lb 14oz	30	2410U	700
5.56x45mm									
H&K HK53	1970	5.56x45	DBB	29.70	8.30	6lb 12oz	25	2460	700
5.7x28mm									
FN P90	1990	5.7x28	BB	19.68	10.35	5lb 9oz	50	2345	900
7.62x25mm Soviet Pistol									
Type 64 Silenced	1964	7.62x25	BB	33.20	9.60	7lb 8oz	30	980	1000
Type 79	1980	7.62x25	Gas	29.13	n/a	4lb 3oz	20	1640	650
Type 85	1985	7.62x25	BB	24.72	n/a	4lb 3oz	30	1640	780
Type 85 Silenced	1985	7.62x25	BB	34.20	9.80	5lb 8oz	30	985	800
CZ24	1951	7.62x25	BB	26.60	11.20	7lb 4oz	32	1800	600
CZ26	1952	7.62x25	BB	27.00	11.20	7lb 4oz	32	1800	600
PPD-34/38	1938	7.62x25	BB	30.70	10.62	8lb 4oz	71	1590	800
PPD-40	1940	7.62x25	BB	30.60	10.63	8lb 2oz	71	1590	800
PPS-42	1942	7.62x25	BB	35.04	10.83	6lb 9oz	35	1590	700
PPS-43	1943	7.62x25	BB	32.28	10.00	7lb 8oz	35	1590	700
PPSh-41	1941	7.62x25	BB	33.00	10.50	8lb	71	1590	900
7.65 Browning									
Skorpion vz61	1960	7.65x17	BB	28.95	4.53	2lb 14oz	20	968	700
7.65mm Longue									
MAS 38	1938	7.65x19	BB	28.90	8.82	6lb 5oz	32	1151	600
8mm Nambu									
Type 100/40	1940	8x21	BB	36.00	9.00	7lb 8oz	30	1100	450
Type 100/44	1944	8x21	BB	36.00	9.20	8lb 8oz	30	1100	800
9mm Short/.380 Auto									
Ingram Model 11	1970	9x17	BB	18.10	5.08	3lb 8oz	32	961	1200

9mm Makarov

Wz-63	1964	9x18	BB	22.95	6.00	3lb 15oz	25	1060	600
PM-84	1983	9x18	BB	22.64	7.28	4lb 9oz	25	1083	600

9mm AUPO

Benelli CB-M2	1980	9x25	BB	26.70	8.10	7lb 2oz	40	1280	1200

9mm Glisenti

Beretta Model 1918	1918	9x19	BB	33.50	21.50	7lb 3oz	25	1250	900
OVP	1920	9x19	BB	35.50	11.00	8lb 1oz	25	1250	900
Villar Perosa	1915	9x19	DBB	21.00	12.50	14lb 6oz	25	1200	1200

9mm Parabellum

Austen Mk 1	1943	9x19	BB	33.25	7.80	8lb 12oz	28	1200	500
Austen Mk 2	1944	9x19	BB	33.25	7.80	8lb 8oz	28	1200	500
Beretta Model 1938A	1938	9x19	BB	37.25	12.40	9lb 4oz	40	1378	600
Beretta Model 38/42	1942	9x19	BB	31.5	8.4	7lb 3oz	40	1250	550
Beretta Model 12	1959	9x19	BB	26.00	7.90	6lb 9oz	40	1250	550
Beretta Model 12S	1983	9x19	BB	26.00	7.80	7lb 1oz	40	1250	550
Bergmann MP18	1916	9x19	BB	32.10	7.80	9lb 3oz	32	1250	400
Bergmann MP28	1928	9x19	BB	32.00	7.80	8lb 13oz	32	1250	650
BXP	1984	9x19	BB	23.90	8.18	5lb 12oz	32	1250	800
Calico M960	1992	9x19	BB	32.87	13.0	4lb 12oz	100	1400	750
Carl Gustav M45	1945	9x19	BB	31.80	8.38	7lb 14oz	36	1345	600
Colt Model RO635	1992	9x19	BB	28.75	10.50	5lb 12oz	32	1300	900
CZ23	1948	9x19	BB	27.00	11.20	6lb 13oz	40	1250	600
CZ25	1948	9x19	BB	27.00	11.20	6lb 13oz	40	1250	600
DUX 53	1953	9x19	BB	32.50	9.84	7lb 11oz	50	1300	500
DUX 59	1959	9x19	BB	31.20	9.84	6lb 10oz	40	1300	550
Erma MPE	1931	9x19	BB	35.04	9.84	9lb 3oz	30	1250	500
Erma MP38	1936	9x19	BB	32.75	9.72	9lb	32	1250	500
Erma MP40	1940	9x19	BB	32.80	9.84	8lb 14oz	32	1250	500
FBP M.48	1948	9x19	BB	32.00	9.80	8lb 3oz	32	1260	500
FBP M.76	1978	9x19	BB	31.50	9.80	6lb 14oz	36	1260	650
Fürrer MP41/44	1943	9x19	Recoil	30.50	9.80	11lb 6oz	40	1312	900
Haenel MP41	1941	9x19	BB	34.05	9.84	8lb 2oz	32	1250	500
H&K MP5A2	1964	9x19	DBB	26.70	8.86	5lb 10oz	30	1312	800
H&K MP5A3	1964	9x19	DBB	26.00	8.86	5lb 10oz	30	1312	800
H&K MP5SD1	1970	9x19	DBB	21.65	5.75	6lb 3oz	30	935	800
H&K MP5SD2	1970	9x19	DBB	30.70	5.75	6lb 13oz	30	935	800
H&K MP5SD3	1970	9x19	DBB	30.70	5.75	7lb 8oz	30	935	800

H&K MP5K	1976	9x19	DBB	12.80	4.52	4lb 6oz	15	1230	900
H&K MP5-PDW	1992	9x19	DBB	31.50	5.50	6lb 3oz	30	1230	900
H&K HK2000	1991	9x19	BB	25.71	–	6lb 3oz	30	1167	880
INDEP Lusa A1	1986	9x19	BB	23.60	6.30	5lb 8oz	30	1280	900
INDEP Lusa A2	1994	9x19	BB	23.00	6.30	6lb 3oz	30	1280	900
Ingram Model 10	1964	9x19	BB	22.0	5.75	6lb	32	1200	1050
Jatimatic	1950	9x19	BB	30.75	7.83	7lb	32	1250	650
Lanchester	1941	9x19	BB	33.50	7.90	9lb 10oz	50	1200	600
Madsen M45	1945	9x19	BB	31.50	12.40	7lb	50	1312	850
Madsen M46	1946	9x19	BB	31.50	7.75	7lb	32	1250	500
Madsen M50	1950	9x19	BB	30.75	7.83	7lb	32	1250	550
Madsen M53	1953	9x19	BB	31.50	7.80	7lb	32	1250	550
MAT 49	1949	9x19	BB	28.35	8.97	7lb 11oz	32	1283	600
Micro-Uzi	1982	9x19	BB	18.11	4.61	4lb 5oz	20	1082	1250
Mini-SAF	1990	9x19	BB	12.20	4.53	5lb 1oz	30	1214	1200
Mini-Uzi	1981	9x19	BB	23.62	7.75	5lb 15oz	32	1155	950
Owen Mk 1	1941	9x19	BB	32.00	9.75	9lb 5oz	33	1378	700
Owen Mk 2	1943	9x19	BB	32.00	9.75	7lb 10oz	33	1378	700
Rexim Favor	1952	9x19	BB	34.35	13.35	10lb 5oz	32	1400	600
SAF	1990	9x19	BB	25.28	7.87	5lb 15oz	30	1280	1200
Schmeisser MK 36	1936	9x19	BB	44.48	19.68	10lb 8oz	25	1350	500
SIG MKPO	1935	9x19	DBB	32.38	11.81	8lb 6oz	30	1312	900
SIG MP310	1958	9x19	BB	28.94	7.87	7lb 9oz	40	1200	900
Sima-Cefar MGP-14	1982	9x19	BB	19.29	6.00	5lb 1oz	32	1122	650
Sima-Cefar MGP-79A	1979	9x19	BB	31.85	9.33	6lb 13oz	32	1345	700
Sima-Cefar MGP-87	1987	9x19	BB	30.16	7.64	6lb 6oz	32	1187	700
Socimi Type 821	1985	9x19	BB	23.62	7.87	5lb 6oz	32	1247	600
Sola Super	1954	9x19	BB	35.00	12.00	6lb 6oz	32	1400	550
Spectre M-4	1985	9x19	BB	22.83	5.12	6lb 6oz	50	1312	850
Star Z-62	1962	9x19	BB	27.60	7.91	6lb 5oz	40	1200	550
Star Z-70/B	1971	9x19	BB	27.60	7.91	6lb 5oz	40	1247	550
Star Z-84	1984	9x19	BB	24.21	8.46	6lb 10oz	30	1312	600
Sten Mk 1	1940	9x19	BB	35.25	7.75	7lb 3oz	32	1250	550
Sten Mk 1*	1941	9x19	BB	31.25	7.80	7lb	32	1250	550
Sten Mk 2	1942	9x19	BB	30.00	7.75	6lb 8oz	32	1250	550
Sten Mk 2S	1942	9x19	BB	35.75	3.50	7lb 12oz	32	1000	450
Sten Mk 3	1942	9x19	BB	30.00	7.75	7lb	32	1250	550
Sten Mk 4	1943	9x19	BB	27.50	3.75	7lb 8oz	32	1200	570
Sten Mk 5	1944	9x19	BB	30.00	7.75	8lb 9oz	32	1250	600

Sten Mk 6	1944	9x19	BB	33.75	3.75	9lb 8oz	32	1000	475
Sterling L2A1	1953	9x19	BB	27.17	7.80	6lb	34	1280	550
Sterling L34A1	1960	9x19	BB	34.02	7.80	7lb 15oz	34	1017	550
Steyr MPi 69/MPi 81	1969	9x19	BB	26.38	10.24	6lb 14oz	32	1250	550
Steyr AUG-9	1986	9x19	BB	26.18	16.54	7lb 5oz	32	1312	700
Steyr TMP	1990	9x19	Recoil	11.10	5.12	2lb 14oz	30	1180	900
Steyr-Solothurn MP34	1930	9x19	BB	33.50	7.75	8lb 8oz	32	1250	500
Suomi M31	1931	9x19	BB	36.02	13.58	9lb 11oz	50	1312	900
United Defense M42	1941	9x19	BB	32.25	11.00	9lb 1oz	20	1312	700
Uzi	1954	9x19	BB	25.60	10.23	8lb 4oz	32	1312	600
Walther MP-K	1963	9x19	BB	25.71	6.73	6lb 3oz	32	1167	550
Walther MP-L	1963	9x19	BB	29.00	10.12	6lb 10oz	32	1300	600
ZK-383	1933	9x19	BB	35.43	12.79	9lb 9oz	30	1250	500/700
9mm Largo									
Star SI-35	1935	9x23	DBB	35.45	10.60	8lb 4oz	40	1350	300/700
Star Z-45	1944	9x23	BB	33.00	7.80	8lb 8oz	30	1250	450
9mm Mauser Export									
Danuvia M39	1939	9x25	DBB	41.25	19.65	8lb 3oz	40	1525	750
Danuvia M43	1943	9x25	DBB	37.50	16.70	8lb	40	1450	750
SIG MKMO	1933	9x25	DBB	40.35	19.68	9lb 4oz	40	1640	900
10mm Auto									
H&K MP5/10	1992	10x25	DBB	26.80	8.86	5lb 14oz	30	1450	800
.40 Smith & Wesson									
H&K MP5/40	1992	.40	DBB	26.80	8.86	5lb 14oz	30	1148	800
.45 ACP									
Hyde-Inland (M2)	1942	.45	BB	32.10	12.10	9lb 4oz	20	960	500
Ingram Model 6	1949	.45	BB	30.00	9.00	7lb 4oz	30	920	600
Ingram Model 10	1964	.45	BB	22.00	5.75	6lb	30	920	1145
Micro-Uzi	1983	.45	BB	18.11	4.61	4lb 5oz	16	787	1000
Thompson M1928A1	1928	.45	DBB	33.75	10.50	10lb 12oz	50	920	700
Thompson M1	1942	.45	BB	32.00	10.50	10lb 7oz	30	920	700
M3	1942	.45	BB	30.00	8.00	8lb 15oz	30	920	450
M3A1	1944	.45	BB	29.75	8.00	8lb 3oz	30	920	450

BB blowback